DEDICATION

To my mother and father, in whom I witnessed strength, compassion, and love. Their lives have made it possible for me to see the character of Christ, who readily gives to those who serve Him. You are my best friends. I love you.

If you think your reward is in heaven and perhaps more stars in your crown or a bigger mansion, you will be disappointed. But when you realize that the reward is Jesus and that heaven itself can offer nothing more, nothing greater, then your reward begins when you enter His service. Through Jesus we enter into rest, so for those working with Him, heaven begins here.

—Morris Venden

CONTENTS

ACKNOWLEDGMENTS

First, I thank Jesus for allowing me to watch while He worked.

Next, I thank Mars (Marilyn Morgan). Without her patience and encouragement, as well as keying in my handwritten manuscript and editing all of it, none of these words would be here.

Thanks also to Cyril and Lyn Connelly and their kids, who took me in like a lost pup, and, just as important, Bob and Myrna Tetz, who are the cohesive force behind the scene.

Chapter 1

AN IDEAL
CHILDHOOD

I first became conscious of the pain and then of the stench of rotten meals and an unflushed toilet. *Where am I?* I blinked, terrified, seeing only four cement walls. Memories of the past night caught up with me as I groaned in anguish. I was busted, lying on a cement bench in a cold cell, wearing nothing but a T-shirt, shorts, and socks. Sitting up stiffly, I still hoped this was a terrible dream, but the reality just kept getting worse. Deep cuts wrapped around both wrists. Handcuffs, I realized.

Stumbling to the sink, I stared into the dull metal mirror, catching a glimpse of something hideous and deplorable. Instead of a smiling blond-haired, blue-eyed young man I expected, a gaunt face surrounded by greasy, stringy hair stared back at me. *What has become of me?* Tears welled up in my eyes, and I had to look away. Stepping over discarded lunchmeat and trying to miss it, I shuffled back to the cold bench. There I curled into a fetal position, and soon the nightmare disappeared in sleep.

Nothing in my childhood portended the road to jail. My early memories smell of orange peels, peanut-butter sandwiches, diesel exhaust, and faint sounds of "Gypsies, Tramps, and Thieves" all wafting through the cold shell of a school bus. Bouncing along the gravel roads of central Alberta, I would melt palm prints in the ice on the windows in order to see the passing snow-covered fields and trees. Endless stops deposited wool-clad kids at their homes.

Our farmhouse nestled among newly planted poplar trees with tractors, trucks, and farm equipment always dotting the landscape. Growing up on a farm was an innocent and whole-some experience. Horses galloped across the pasture, cows grazed lazily, and dogs always looked for affection.

I am a third-generation Seventh-day Adventist (SDA). My grandfather moved from the Dakotas in the late 1800s to Canada and began farming—the only life he'd ever known. We were totally dependent on the land and at the mercy of the elements. My father, Llewellyn, took over from his dad, and he hoped that my brother and I would take over the farm from him. Farming often is a handed-down business, and most sons cherish the day when they receive their birthright. With two sons, Dad thought he'd have a taker. But it was not to be.

When I began grade one in a public school in the little town of Mirror, I encountered worldly influences for the first time. Frankie Brown hated me for some reason and constantly chased me. Class bully, big and fortunately slow, he'd holler and spout off mouthfuls of swear words—words I'd never heard before but came to understand were a part of the world.

The next year my parents made a decision to pull us out of public school and drive us each day to an Adventist school twenty-five miles away at what was then called Canadian Union College (CUC). While twenty-five miles may not seem far, fighting bone-chilling temperatures and impassible snowdrifts in the winter took its toll.

The following year my parents made another decision. They sold the farm and moved into a farmhouse five miles from the town of Lacombe and the college. I didn't realize the sacrifice they made to provide my Christian education but did recognize their desire for it.

I liked my new surroundings, friends, and school. No more Frankie Brown. Our neighbors had two girls who went to the same school, so we carpooled. No more smelly buses or long rides across the prairie. My mom or dad woke me every morning and, after I washed my face, brushed my teeth, and finished dressing, I'd sit quietly at the breakfast table, listening to one of them read from our daily devotional book and then pray. Both of my parents, dedicated Christians, gave everything they had to educate me in the truths of Jesus Christ.

Outgoing and popular, always involved, and excelling in every sport, I found elementary school a blast. Grade nine graduation came with a trophy for best athlete, and I felt on top of the world.

Money was tight even though Dad continued to farm some land in the area. I remember listening to Mom and Dad talk in hushed voices at the table. Mom, with the accounting books open, and Dad, with a worried look, said, "We just can't afford it."

My mom, Marlene, replied, "But we have to do it."

"It'll be OK. The Lord will provide," responded my dad.

Listening in the shadows, I felt tightness in my chest that almost kept me from breathing. *What are they talking about?* I wondered. *Is it me? Am I costing too much?*

"We can't lose the house. I'll find a way." My dad's whispers consoled my worried mom.

Oh no! I gasped inside. *What are we going to do?* My stomach churned, and I crept silently back to my room. Off and on I caught remarks pertaining to our lack of money. My childish imagination pictured poverty and homelessness even though I never went to bed hungry, and what we may have lacked in money, my folks made up for in love. Their huge sacrifices for my education and Christian upbringing only made my memories more painful when years later I found myself sick, detoxing from drugs, and lying on the floor of a county jail thousands of miles from that innocent life.

In my first year of high school, still at CUC, I began experimenting with alcohol. As a kid I'd tried smoking and had hated

11

it. I drank once at a neighbor's place on a sleepover but never felt interested. I knew I'd crush my parents' hearts if they found out. High school brought new friends and also new temptations, and here I began experimenting with pot and booze. I wanted to try everything and had no fear of consequences—only guilt about my parents' concern.

When I began playing sports in the town league, I met another group of people. Growing up on a farm and attending CUC had kept me sheltered from the world around. Associating only with Adventists hadn't given me any experience with "outsiders." But the town league exposed me to a new world, a world without Friday evening curfews and Sabbath boredom, a world without all the "No you can'ts" and plenty of "It's OKs."

Living as an Adventist but playing baseball as a town kid gave me questions without answers. *Why are they allowed to play on Saturday?* I'd wonder out loud sometimes. *Why can't I listen to that music? Why do they eat pork?* Internalizing many of these questions and afraid to ask for fear of disappointing my parents, I said nothing. Even at that young age, I could feel the pull of the world, the tearing away of Christian standards so painstakingly set up and nurtured.

Although I enjoyed an ideal childhood with every opportunity to be a winner for Christ, I began slipping gradually into an abyss that would lead to destruction. Satan, slow and patient, always taking, taking, taking, eroded the foundation my parents sacrificed for. Playing baseball, showing horses, joining the 4-H club, playing in the band, performing on the gymnastics team— all these activities my loving parents paid for with no strings attached, only hoping to guide a rosy-cheeked, bright child into adulthood without too much pain.

Instead, peering through my small window and out across no-man's-land, surrounded by an electric fence and razor wire and gun towers, I now write from a cement box I call home at High Desert State Prison in Susanville, California.

Chapter 2

BORN
TO SELL

From a very young age, I always had a head for business. Something about selling gave me pleasure, whether from the profit gained from the sale or the power felt during the exchange of money, I don't know. But one thing is certain—I was born to sell.

In grade six a friend of mine and I hatched a plan to capitalize on the needs of a few students after a memo circulated saying that chewing gum would not be allowed during school. Many of the kids lived in the country, so school was their only chance to obtain chewing gum, which was given to them by those from town. In those days gum cost twenty cents a pack, and each pack had five pieces in all sorts of colorful flavors.

My partner, Mick, and I had to be covert, so we hollowed out two dictionaries, carrying them everywhere toting our illegal stash. To the teachers we may have appeared like overzealous English students, but students knew what we had when they saw the dictionaries.

We sold each piece for twenty cents and soon had everyone in school, or so it seemed, buying gum. Mick lived in town, but I lived on a farm, so each afternoon he rode his bike to the store and restocked our supply. Soon we each had a handful of change and then a little stack of bills. Wow! We were big shots, breaking the law and making a profit. But in most illegal enterprises, someone gets caught and to save themselves, they tell the higher-ups. And so it was with my first attempt to get rich quick.

I always had my eyes open for ways to make money. Living on the farm presented occasional opportunities for profit, and I quickly jumped at every chance. Chores, the daily feeding and watering of our horses and cows every evening after school, were just part of daily life. They took only an hour or two, but I'd often envy my friends in town who were free to do as they pleased after school.

Seeing my lack of enthusiasm, Dad often spiced up things with the number one motivator—money. In the summer my dad and brother bailed hay. The bales had to be lying the right way in order to be picked up by the loader. So my dad paid me a dollar for each bale I had to straighten. Readers might think the pay low as they picture a young boy wandering over hundreds of acres straightening bales. Let me clear the scene. Picture a young boy riding a late model dirt bike screaming through row after row of bales hoping to find one to turn over. A thoughtful boy probably would have understood that dirt bikes and gas weren't free—neither were food, clothes, tuition, and a roof overhead—but to me, money equaled happiness.

One year while my brother and I were in 4-H, my father allowed us each to pick out a calf. We were to learn how to care for and nurture animals. All winter I monitored my calf's feed and supplements, carefully logging the various information. But I thought only about how much money I'd get when spring came and the calf would be auctioned off, sold by the pound. While the other kids had formed bonds with their calves and struggled through tears when the auction started, I couldn't wait to see my check.

Having learned to ride horses when very young, after grade nine I applied for my first real job at a summer camp in British Columbia. Those students who worked there earned a scholarship, and I liked the idea of getting away from the farm for a summer. The director hired me as the horse wrangler. Taking care of the camp's horses, giving trail rides, and teaching horsemanship was a blast made even better when, after some begging, my dad consented to send my own purebred show horse to camp with me. Towering above the riffraff trail ponies, I rode like someone important, never stopping to think that it probably cost as much to send my horse to British Columbia and back as the scholarship I earned. But Dad never said a word.

Next summer I applied for a job at the Color Press, a business on campus where my mother worked part time as a bookkeeper. The job was hell, or so I kept telling myself. Fixed wage, no incentives, and about as boring as could be. I hated it—almost enough to ask Dad if I could quit the press and work for him. Even sitting, hot and sweaty, on the tractor would've been a treat, but my pride didn't let me quit. I secretly hoped to be fired, but no such luck. Working for a wage didn't motivate me. I'd often wonder how so many people could get up every morning day after day knowing that at the end of the day all they could look forward to was another day like the previous one.

I wasn't lazy. I'd work for a dollar if I had an incentive, but punching a clock wasn't for me. Always looking to make a buck soon brought me my first brush with the law.

Several years later, in high school, a few kids experimented with pot. Although I had tried it, I wasn't enthusiastic about it; it mostly just made me tired and paranoid. I feared getting caught—my hide wouldn't have fared too well if that had happened. But the "risk versus profit" factor snares the greedy every time. So with money on my mind, I stole a jar of parsley from my mom's spice cupboard, bought some rolling papers, and began an illegal operation, "Project Parsley," knowing the worst outcome would be making a few guys upset when they discovered they weren't choking on pot.

But to my surprise, the day after selling veggie joints, the guys called me back and wanted more—an unexpected turn of events. My first taste of almost being a drug dealer ended pretty well, or so I thought. Then one day the dean called me into his office. There sat the dean, assistant dean, and my brother, the resident assistant for the men's dorm. By the expressions on their faces, I knew the visit wouldn't be pleasant. Suddenly, my mouth went dry, and my heart pounded as I stood, terrified. Ironically, the dry mouth, weakness, and terror would visit me time and time again over the next ten years.

The dean didn't pull punches. "Sit down, Rick," he said in a quiet voice. Shaking, I surveyed the scene. The dean sat behind a desk too big for the room, staring at me intently, hands clasped into a fist on the desk. The assistant dean and gymnastics chaplain, my good friend, sat in an overstuffed, old-fashioned armchair, hands squarely on the armrests, shoulders straight. I searched their faces. My eyes finally fell on my brother's face, whose look I didn't want to leave. Compassion and love, loyalty and defiance resonated from him. Facing the three of them, I sat on a stool positioned in the center of the room.

"Rick, we know you've been selling drugs . . ."

Oh, God, please get me out of this, I prayed silently, and ironically would plead this same prayer many times in the years to come. *Lord, if You get me out of this one, I'll never do it again.* But amazingly, God answered my foxhole prayers time and time again.

". . . and selling drugs is a felony. You could be arrested, Rick." He paused.

"And, furthermore, you'd be expelled from school and also be kicked off the gymnastics team," the assistant interjected. I looked at him with tears in my eyes. Beads of sweat rolled down my back. *What can I do? What can I say?* My mind polled every conceivable explanation. I continued to pray, now terrified of the consequences.

"What do you think your parents will say?" The dean knew exactly what would hit the hardest.

Tears streamed down my face, my brother's too. "I didn't do it!" I blurted out between sobs. "You guys are wrong. I swear I didn't do it."

Instantly, as if on cue, my brother, who'd been quiet until now, spoke up. "You heard him, and I believe him. Dean, he didn't do it—if he said he didn't, then he didn't."

"I didn't, I really didn't . . ." my voice trailed off.

The deans, with resigned looks on their faces, knowing they had no real evidence and not really wanting to kick me out anyway, let this encounter be one of learning, not punishing. "OK, Rick, we're giving you one more chance. You're free to go." I walked out unscathed, feeling as if I had won the lottery—and soon forgot every regret and fear I had while under fire. I began to rationalize that nothing was illegal unless I got caught and charged.

Having always received good grades in school, I decided college was the obvious choice, so I first attended Newbold College, a little Adventist school in England. The allure of living in a foreign country persuaded my friend Vic and me to try something different.

Once past the excitement and adjustment of living in a foreign country, Vic and I quickly transformed our ideas of learning into lounging and spent most of the week going to London or visiting every neighborhood pub we could find. We stocked the shelves in the dorm room with liquor and beer, and even rigged up a hair dryer to blow our cigarette smoke out the window to avoid getting caught by the dean.

My first run-in with the staff occurred when I failed to show up for work. The curriculum included an assigned job a few hours a week, and I had been assigned to horticulture. But no way did I intend to pull and not get paid. "Have they lost their minds?" I wondered out loud to Vic. Soon I found myself sitting in front of the college president, Dr. Sakae Kubo.

"Rick, are you having trouble with your job assignment?" he questioned kindly.

"No, there's really no problem. I just am not going to do it," I replied matter-of-factly, expecting to spark an argument. But none came.

Dr. Kubo sat quietly before he spoke again. "Rick, here at Newbold we have some requirements which you, as a student, are expected to fulfill. Student work not only helps with the upkeep of the school, but it gives you a purpose and goal, helping your education."

He paused, and I seized the opportunity. "I'm not working in some greenhouse digging around in the dirt for free. I come from a farm, I hate farming, and I won't weed for anybody!"

Waiting for an angry response, I braced myself. "Well, Rick, I can see your point. I see you have an issue specifically with horticulture, so if I reassign you, will you work?" he said without so much as raising his voice.

I sat amazed at Dr. Kubo's demeanor. He was so polite, kind, and genuine that I couldn't continue my tirade. "What do you have in mind, sir?"

"Well, I need a janitor here to do a little work helping me take out the trash and to clean up. Would that be OK?"

What could I say? He was so nice, and I knew he had bent over backward to placate me. "OK, sir, I'll do it—and thanks for being understanding," I said as I walked out.

How could he be so nice when I acted so rudely? I wondered to myself, not yet understanding how God works. Even when railed against and taunted, Dr. Kubo stayed patient, giving me a true Christian example. But eventually I persuaded myself that his kindness was really weakness and barely set foot in his office again to do the work I'd promised to do.

That quarter came to a close, and because of my partying and skipping school, I had earned only one credit—for fine arts. The course had entailed riding on a bus every Thursday looking at English architecture. I used the time to catch up on sleep. How oblivious I was to the opportunity my dear parents were working so hard to give me. But my irresponsibility didn't end there.

The next year I talked another friend into going to Washington State with me to attend Walla Walla College. Another attempt, another opportunity, and another bundle of cash thrown away. After the first quarter ended, the college dean asked me not to return—no surprise to me. I hadn't really attended college anyway.

Chapter 3

PITCHMAN

Some time later a friend of mine saw a streak of cockiness in me that he deemed ideal for the business of pitchman, a business that has been around for centuries. Snake-oil salesmen have bilked multitudes out of money for centuries. Something about watching a person who looks so convinced that he's got the cure for everything and sells it at a pittance, makes people buy.

People flock to the demo stands at county fairs, exhibitions, and home shows. In the past, barkers would frequently be run out of town and only by sheer luck miss being lynched by angry mobs that had bought their cure-alls, only to find them just pretty bottles of nothing. Today's pitchmen are much more educated in the art, and instead of selling a completely useless item, they sell things some folks actually like.

I got my first opportunity just out of high school selling a blender that could make peanut butter, coleslaw, and all kinds of healthful juices. My friend Bob, who'd been pitching the blender for a couple of years, put in a good word with the owner, who had been looking for a second pitchman to work the summer fair circuit. Walter Honke, a tall German man, and his lovely wife, Aida, hired me. He'd been selling blenders for thirty years and knew talent when he saw it.

I reported to work a couple days after high school graduation. The "summer run," as we called it, consisted of five fairs in western Canada. Walter paid one hundred dollars a day, cash. Forty-eight days, forty-eight hundred dollars—more than I'd ever made in a summer. Forty-eight hundred dollars! I couldn't believe my luck.

The fairs varied from six to ten days, but the big one, Vancouver, was seventeen days long. I couldn't wait! The first couple of days were rocky, but once I'd memorized the fifteen-minute pitch, coordinated my words with the motions of making the drinks, I was off and running. I was made for this business, where I stood in front of crowds, microphone blaring, the center of attention. When the day ended, other pitchmen and I often stopped at a bar, ate, and had a drink or two.

Walter warned me, "Rick, I don't want you guys hanging around with any of the other pitchmen? They're into hard drugs and group sex. Stay away from them!"

I didn't question him. *After all, he's been in the business for thirty years, so he should know what he's talking about,* I told myself. But when I had a chance, I asked Bob, "What's the deal with these other pitchmen? Are they really bad news like Walter said?"

"Yeah, some of them are, but Walter just doesn't want us hanging with them because we might get ideas of going to work for them."

"Why would I do that? I'm making a hundred bucks a day!"

Bob's eyes narrowed. "That's peanuts compared to most."

Stunned, I noticed Bob's tone and didn't pursue the conversation. *Peanuts,* I thought to myself. *One hundred bucks is peanuts? Not where I'm from!*

Later on that summer while I sat in the exhibitor's lounge having a sandwich, a pitchman named Larry sat down beside me. "How are you doing?" He smiled, holding a beer.

"Fine, thanks," I replied.

"Wow, some day, huh?" he said sipping on the cold, golden liquid.

"Yeah, I guess it's OK, about the same as all of them, don't you think?"

"Oh, heck, no," he said shaking his head. "I'm going to double what I sold yesterday—should be able to pull down five hundred dollars today."

"Five hundred dollars?" I stammered.

"Yep."

"For yourself?" I choked.

"Yep," he smiled and sat back, lighting a cigarette.

I'd lost my appetite at this point and began a rookie interrogation, much to Larry's delight. "Wait a minute. How'd you make five hundred dollars in one day?" I demanded, thinking he was lying.

"I get paid commission, a percentage of everything I sell. Don't you?" he asked matter-of-factly.

"No." I shook my head. Larry and all the other pitchmen knew Walter paid one hundred a day (actually, one hundred dollars a day in 1983 for an eighteen-year-old kid was really good money). Larry must have been crying with laughter watching the wheels turn as I did the math in my head. We averaged twenty blenders a day. Each one sold for one hundred eighty dollars plus attachments, coming to around two hundred dollars. After a minute of silence I said, "How much is your percentage?"

"Twenty-five points, Buddy. I wouldn't work for less." He smiled and got up. "See ya around, Kid. Have a good show."

I nodded and smiled, but inside I boiled. Twenty-five percent of four thousand split between Bob and me equaled five hundred dollars a day. Somehow the hundred I was making didn't seem as good anymore. I decided right then that I would one day work a booth for some real money.

The next year I asked Walter if he'd pay me a percentage—not a big one, just 15 percent. "I've been doing this for thirty years, never paid any points to my workers, and never will," he responded. The finality in his voice assured me that no matter how good I might be, he'd never be swayed. So, driven by my unquenchable thirst for money, I jumped ship when another offer came along.

After a couple of years, I moved on to smaller-ticket items that sold by the truckloads: car chamois, vegetable slicers, cheese graters—all kinds of gadgets that people bought on impulse, usually due to the pitchman's story and smile. Time and time again people came to my booth and told me they had bought some gadget last year or the year before. I'd hold my breath, examine their body language to see if they were going to swing at me or hug me, and as soon as I picked up their attitude, I'd instantly go into action. If a person was angry, I'd shut off the microphone and be Dr. Phil, consoling and soothing the upset buyer, promising to make it up to him or her.

First, I offered them a quick review on how to use it, asking if they had read the instructions. Most people would say No, and then I had them. "Oh, you didn't read the instructions," I'd say after quickly turning the microphone back on. "Well, you just sit back and let me give you a free refresher course." Their demeanor would change as the word *free* sank in, and my hands would fly over the counter reorganizing it for a show, talking all the while. The once-disgruntled customer would stand there while a crowd began to build. I'd start into the pitch, both guns blazing, oftentimes cutting the same vegetable over and over just babbling until the crowd swelled to its largest. Then I'd do the magical cut that only my machine could do. People's eyes would widen. Some mouths would drop open, and the women would nudge one another, nodding in agreement about how wonderful their lives would be if they had one of those machines.

By this time the disgruntled person would be fully back in the state of mind of the year before when she vowed to herself she couldn't live without the gadget I was selling. Time and time again that same person who originally came to give me an earful suddenly felt the need to buy another one!

Drawing to the end of the pitch, I always used the "fear and greed" factor. Everyone has heard the famous banter, "I have only a few of these left . . ." or "Buy it now before I run out . . ." or "Order now and save money. . . ." These lies draw out greed in people. Obviously, if I'm at a booth selling a product, I'd be an idiot to run out and squander many remaining days of sale. But nevertheless, when the demo was finished and it was time to ask for money, I'd say it time and again. Done right, I'd feel the same rush every time while watching people push and shove each other to get to the front and buy one of the last few.

I never ceased to be amazed, while watching people dig in their pockets or purses, how much power words and suggestions have. People will follow one another like sheep. If one buys, many will buy, and that's what the once-disgruntled customer is for. Now with the crowd securely around her, I'd ask if anyone had bought my miracle machine before—looking out into the crowd, I would see in my peripheral vision a hand poking up right in front. "Oh, you have. Isn't that wonderful! Oh, what's that? You want another one for your daughter-in-law? My, my, I wish my mother-in-law were this pleasant, don't you? Ha! Ha!" and with that the frenzied buyers would elbow their way to the front waving twenty dollar bills in my face. Like picking flowers in a field, I'd exchange those bills for the gadgets soon to be collecting dust in their cupboards.

Many people buy on impulse. To help our fellow pitchmen, we'd use transparent bags for our merchandise. Not only did they advertise for us when others saw the gadgets in the bags, but for the next pitchman down the line, the bags revealed gullible potential customers.

One day a pitchman whom I respected for his talent and skill pulled me aside and asked if I could find him some pot. Because I knew a few people, I said I'd look around. Later I picked up a bag and walked to his Ginsu® knife booth, where he had dozens of wide-eyed people mesmerized by the flashing blade making unbelievable cuts on vegetables and fruit. As I watched I, too, became impressed by his energy, charisma, and stamina. Fairs and exhibitions are long and hard, but he looked as fresh as if he'd just awakened. After a flurry of money exchanging hands, the crowd left with their indestructible Ginsu knives.

Tony jumped off the booth and motioned for me to follow him to the public restrooms and then into a stall. He took the one next to me, and I heard him lock the door, so I did the same. Next I saw a wad of bills under the partition. I took them, dug out the bag of pot, and handed it back under the grimy, graffiti-covered stall partition. *Wow, I'm doing a drug deal!* The fact hit me right then. It gave me a sense of heightened pleasure, the same rush as on the pitch booth but multiplied by the illegality and potential risk of getting busted.

I thought we were finished when I saw his hand under the stall again with a small glass gadget about the size of a lipstick tube. It sat there in his hand, and I guess he got tired of waiting, so he whispered, "Do you want some or what?" I took it, not wanting to look stupid but feeling exactly that. It had a little knob on the side, so I turned the knob, and a small stream of white powder fell onto the dirty floor. My mind whirled as I tried to figure out what it was, how it worked, and whether I should be holding this strange-looking contraption. I must have taken a moment too long, or possibly Tony was just scared and didn't want to be in a smelly public toilet holding a bag of pot and snorting cocaine. He whispered again, "Go ahead; help yourself."

So hardly knowing what I was doing, I put the thing up to my nose, gave the knob a twist, and drew in a healthy snort. Instantly I felt the sting of something foreign in my throat and nose. I gagged but thrust it into my other nostril. Quickly I shoved the gadget back to Tony, wondering just what I'd done. I had told myself I wasn't going to do coke, but that promise to myself was now broken. Coming out of the stall, I followed Tony to the sink and mirror and mimed him as he tilted his head back, making sure no telltale powder showed. Sniffing deeply a few times as my nose began to run and my throat began to numb, I shook hands, and we parted ways.

I walked back to my booth just in time for the last hour of work and suddenly felt alive. Only minutes before I had been tired and looking forward to the end of the day. But now I was loud, animated, and rolling as if it were 10:00 A.M. instead of 10:00 P.M. I couldn't believe how upbeat I felt. People were laughing and buying—and I was on top of the world. This feeling didn't end when the people left, so I went out and partied like never before, feeling invincible. Little did I know what madness I'd just bought into. Pandora's box had been opened, and the kid with all the potential, charm, and natural ability would soon become another victim in the long line of drug abusers. For the next few days until the fair was over, I'd mosey down to Tony's knife booth, wait until he was off, go to the same stall, and repeat the same process. My sales went way up, and everyone was happy. From that point on, I did cocaine every chance I could. Fortunately, in Canada it was expensive and hard to find, preventing me from crashing and burning much sooner.

Not everyone I worked with used drugs. Pitchmen are a close-knit group who travel from show to show, state to state, hotel to hotel, often staying at the same places year after year. Many times rumors of my conduct surfaced, and older pitchmen would give me a scolding or a backhanded comment. I'd just laugh and pretend they were kidding, assuring them they had nothing to worry about. Bill Latoske, a man I greatly respected, played a part in my wake-up call, and, in return, through the unseen hand of God, I was later used to play a part in his.

My insatiable desire for money, travel, and nightlife made studying impossible, so I buried the notion of a degree in biology and the hope of becoming a dentist. I lived only for the moment. Making no claim on sanity, I dove into the rat race of making money and sacrificing whatever it took to get rich.

Chapter 4

DIRTY
LITTLE SECRET

I began working for a company out of Seattle selling an all-purpose chamois cloth. Go to any fair or swap meet nowadays and you'll see the brilliantly colored synthetic cloths stacked high on a counter. The pitchmen pour water on a black vinyl pad and then with a magical swipe, the super chamois picks it all up. Originally from Germany, these towels sold like hotcakes. I was fortunate enough to land a job selling them in many summer fairs. Now, working on commission and getting 25 percent of every chamois I sold, I thought nothing could stop me.

My boss and owner of the company, Kenny, was one in a million. We hit it off right from the start. He partied; I partied. He worked hard; I worked hard. Side by side we'd spin our pitches to the masses selling these orange towels for ten dollars, laughing inside knowing they cost only a buck. Kenny and I would switch each hour. He'd work one, then I'd work one, alternating throughout the day. Some of the fair buildings were sweltering hot, so Kenny would bring in a cooler packed with ice and beer. I always thought it was strange to have a boss who encouraged drinking booze while working—but being young and full of life, I loved the challenge.

Then one day I noticed some white powder on the box under the counter. Running my finger over the powder, then rubbing it on my gums, which instantly turned numb, I knew what was up. Kenny did coke. *Wow. What luck,* I thought to myself as I felt the excitement build in my chest. *I can get coke from my boss. How convenient.*

As soon as I saw him, I pulled him into the back room behind our booth. "Kenny, I want in . . ." leaving him to figure out what I was talking about. He stood there with a puzzled look on his face.

"What do you mean, Rick?" he said in his unmistakable southern drawl.

"I need some pick-me-up, Kenny, and don't mind paying for it," I said staring at his dilated pupils.

He paused, then shrugged. "OK, you're in. I'll take it out of your pay."

With that he pulled out a small baggie and split the contents in two. "Get to work; let's make some money, Buddy," he said over his shoulder as he sauntered out of the room disappearing down the crowded aisle.

Mesmerized by the sparkling powder, I chopped out a tiny line and scraped it from side to side. Every nerve in my body tingling, I pulled a crisp bill out of my wad and meticulously rolled it up ritualistically, exaggerating every move. Then I thrust one end in my nose and the other in the pile and snorted hard, filling first one nostril and then the other. Doing my own coke somehow felt different. I now had a friend in coke that I could use when I needed to make that extra sale. I vowed to use it only when needed and sparingly. *It is a tool, an aid to help me sell— and nothing more,* I lied to myself. Little did I know the tables would turn, and soon I would no longer be using it—it would be using me.

At the end of that summer, Kenny invited me to his house for a few days to relax, eat, and discuss the fall shows. He and his wife, Sherri, owned a beautiful home in a nice neighborhood. The house, filled with toys only good money could buy, was impressive. After figuring out my wages, he told me to go to the garage, look in the freezer, and grab any one of the brown bags at the bottom. Puzzled, I went to the garage, opened the freezer, and chose one of the six or seven grocery bags sitting in the frosty enclosure. I sat with wide-eyed unbelief as Kenny tipped the bag upside down and bundles of neatly wrapped bills spilled onto the dining room table, with some hitting the floor. I'd never seen so much cash in all my life—thousands upon thousands of literally cold, hard cash.

Kenny laughed, "So you think you want to be a pitchman, huh?"

I was speechless, but inside I knew I'd found the pot of gold at the end of the rainbow. This was only one of many bags in that freezer—I was in awe. Kenny stacked up ten bundles in front of me. "Count 'em, Kid. Make sure I ain't stiffin' ya any," he instructed, enjoying the starstruck look of a young man with a plan. Kenny was a motivator. He knew greed; it stared him in the face every morning just like it did the rest of us. I was hooked on everything about Kenny. The next morning, after Sherri went to run errands, Kenny called me into the kitchen. I watched as he pulled out a little baggie of coke, "Watcha say we have a little celebration, Rick? This one's on me."

He smiled, and I nodded as I cracked a beer and pulled up a seat next to the counter, waiting for him to pour out a pile, get out a credit card, and begin chopping it into lines. But this time was different. Kenny reached into the silverware drawer and pulled out a spoon, giving it a slight bend to even out the scoop.

"What are you doing?" I said inquisitively.

He didn't respond but as if in a trance continued the strange setup. Next, he filled a cup with water, setting it beside the spoon, and then set a cotton ball beside the spoon and water. Puzzled, I remained quiet, taking it all in. The next thing I saw tied this whole strange ritual together. Out of his shirt pocket came a small syringe. My mouth dropped open. "Oh, no way, Kenny. What are you going to do with that?" I said barely believing my eyes. *A junkie? Kenny's a junkie?* I said to myself.

As I watched him load the syringe and slam it into his vein, I was frightened by the sight and recoiled in disgust. *How can so much success and money follow a junkie?* I wondered as I watched him shoot himself into another dimension. I don't know how my mind changed so quickly, how the disgust turned into curiosity or fear morphed into desire. But within an hour I, too, was lost, shot into another dimension like Kenny, crossing yet another line I'd sworn never to cross. I felt dirty but rationalized that if Kenny did drugs like that without anyone knowing, and he was successful, then why couldn't I do the same?

From then on it became my dirty little secret—most pitchmen steered clear of junkies, so I kept it quiet, not wanting to end up blacklisted and unable to work. I should have recognized the true devastation of drug abuse when only a couple years later Kenny lost everything. His wife found out, and he disappeared into the streets, living out of a car, begging for money.

Chapter 5

THE

EDGE

C'mon, Vic. Let's get out of here," I said wearily. Four weeks of drug-laced partying mixed with work had left both of us exhausted and gaunt. Vic, my boyhood friend, and I had worked the spring home show in Vancouver, British Columbia, selling chamois cloths for use in homes and cars.

The show had been a dud, and the little money we did make we spent on cocaine and the lifestyle that goes with it. Lifting my suitcase into the trunk, I could feel the soreness in my arms. I felt sick knowing the ache didn't come from hard work but from the black-and-blue tracks up and down my veins. Night after night I had slammed cocaine into my veins for a momentary rush that only took me deeper every time it ended. I thought to myself, *How did you end up doing something so stupid? You're a junkie living in a yuppie's body.*

Shutting the trunk of my sleek black sports car, I tried to clear my head. *I've got to get out of here,* I told myself silently.

The overcast sky threatened rain—March in Vancouver, British Columbia, equals rain. Not that I'd noticed. Some days I managed to find a couple hours of drunken sleep, but I always awoke looking for another drink to kill the night-before pain. I'd get up at 1:00 P.M., stumble around, shower, take some pills or

31

smoke a joint, wander down to the hotel coffee shop, look into a cup of coffee, and wonder how much worse life could get.

To an onlooker, I might have appeared normal: They might have assumed at a glance that I was a young, clean-cut guy on his way to success, but they didn't see the blackened heart and mind—truly a walking lie.

Work had been a series of plays acted on a display booth—a canned spiel demonstrating the hundreds of uses for this yellow cloth. Smiling at the crowd, I'd drone on and on, hoping to sell some. Every dollar meant another drink or another drug. Ten o'clock couldn't come soon enough. Often we'd already be drunk before work ended.

In the morning while still sick from the night before, I would swear that that evening I would go straight to my room to sleep. No partying. But about 6:00 P.M., after a couple drinks and maybe a shot of cocaine, my resolution would weaken. *I can do it. I can go out for just one drink, just one, no big deal. I'll be asleep by eleven, plenty of time for a good night's sleep,* I'd lie to myself day after day.

Hotel life fostered my addictions—every evening I came back to a clean room devoid of empty beer cans, filthy ashtrays, and dirty needles from the night before. It's impossible to understand how I could forget the feelings of the morning. But night after night I'd turn from being the boy next door to being the creepy thing in the cellar, and morning after morning I'd swear, "Never again."

But that memory faded quickly when I headed out of Vancouver and, I hoped, out of the nightmare. A light drizzle misted the windows as the high-rises receded in my mirror. Driving through the orchards and lush green pastures of Abbotsford, I headed east for Calgary, Alberta, ten hours away.

Smoking a cigarette, I checked out the raccoonlike circles around my eyes and sunken cheeks staring back at me in the mirror. *What a mess I am,* I thought. Looking at Vic sleeping in the passenger seat, I wondered if he ever felt the same way. We both came from good homes and had all the opportunities needed to succeed; yet, here we sat, chasing a pot of gold, yet settling for hangovers and needle marks. What separated us from the junkie pushing a shopping cart in the back alley? Facade, that's all. At heart we're the same. Little did I know that in a few hours my life would take a devastating turn, and in a few more years an even deadlier one.

The miles rolled past all the beautiful mountain scenes. Highway 1 winds through some of the most spectacular stretches of the Canadian Rockies. The rain stopped, and a cool mountain breeze whispered over my little black two-seater. What a sweet little car—high-performance engine, spoiler, ground effects, fat tires, and all the bells and whistles. The Pontiac Fierro GT wasn't really mine, though. Actually, the bank owned it, and at the moment I was a couple of payments late, but who knew? Again, all part of the show.

Eventually, evening came and with it the demons. The stereo pumped loud party tunes as Vic and I sipped beer bought somewhere along the way. Like every other day, my addiction forced me to plot how to score some drugs. Silly idea at first, but as the miles evaporated, the thought, once germinated, grew, and soon we discussed the possibilities. Getting out the map, we found the next large city to be an hour away, and before long we had talked ourselves into looking around. *Large* is an overstatement for Kamloops, British Columbia, but it had a couple of bars, and we knew that with bars come drugs.

After a couple of hours and several different bars, we found what we were looking for—cocaine and a house party when the bars closed. Hours later we sat once again side by side. "What do you want to do, Vic?" I slurred.

"I don't know . . ." he mumbled.

"Are you tired?" I asked.

"No."

"Can you drive?"

"Yes."

"Then let's get out of here," I said as we switched seats. Tired and drunk, I found that the cocaine wasn't good enough to keep me awake. After a month of daily abuse, my body's tolerance had peaked.

At 3:00 A.M. I awoke to freezing wind blasting through the window. "What are you doing?" I yelled at Vic.

"I'm getting some fresh air to wake me up. I'm feeling tired," he spat back. "Do you want to drive?'

"No."

"Then shut up and go back to sleep."

Rolling to my side, I unfastened the seat belt for comfort, curled up against the door, and dozed off again.

Majestic cliffs shot skyward on one side; a steep embankment fell away on the other. Water from the spring snowmelt had carved deep ridges that ran down the embankment. Still lightly covered with snow, these ridges were lethal. As the car rounded a curve, a rolling, jerky sensation woke me. "Vic! Vic! Look out!" His closed eyes opened and his hands jerked the wheel—but too late. With the back tires sliding sideways, the car was instantly out of control. Drifting perpendicular to the ridges initially felt like a smooth side-to-side motion, but when the tires caught the frozen ridges, it felt like hitting a street curb sideways at sixty miles per hour. The ridges flipped the car into a barrel roll, then, somehow, end over end. Helpless, we were at fate's mercy. I say "fate" because at that point in my life God was anything but a friend. God, on the other hand, had a different plan.

One, two, three times we rocked side to side. Then everything went dark and quiet. A drowning feeling began to overtake me.

"Help me, help me! Vic! Where are you? Help! Help! Oh, God, help!" The words gurgled out of my mouth through bubbles of blood. My body felt cold, and I couldn't move. Although my eyes were wide open, I couldn't see. A sick, drowning feeling began to overcome me. I gasped for air, but each breath brought blood with it.

"Vic, Vic, help me," I whispered as my voice began to fail.

"I'm here. I'm here. Rick, I'm so sorry, so sorry. You're going to be OK. I'm here. I'm here."

His voice sounded labored. He knelt in the snow and held my head up. "I'm blind. I can't see. Why can't I see? Help me," I continued to plead.

For an instant my eyes focused, and I looked around, quickly trying to see what had happened. The car lay a hundred or so feet away on its wheels nosed into a small stand of trees that skirted a cliff. I could see the shape of my car's hood and top embedded in the snow, but the flipping car left only outlines of its body in the otherwise pristine layer of snow. My body was pressed into one of those outlines because I had been ejected through the sunroof and then the car had landed on top of me during one of its several flips. The weight of the car had crushed me, and now I lay badly injured in the snow.

"Vic, I'm dying. I know I'm dying. Tell my folks I love them. Vic, I don't want to die. Vic . . ." My voice trailed off as I struggled to breathe. I remember thinking of all the things I wanted to do but now wouldn't have the chance. No goodbyes. No apologies. Nothing but death. What would happen? I knew I wasn't saved, but I couldn't care less about God. I wasn't even sure He existed. But, ironically, I'd been yelling His name. The biting cold left my body numb, and I was dying.

What a sad sight! A young man barely into his twenties lying in a broken heap, body ravaged by drugs, and barely alive. Helpless and hopeless, I lay completely at the mercy of the Author of life. Fading into unconsciousness, I faintly heard a voice. "Hello down there." Then another. "Are you OK?"

Vic yelled back, "Help us; help us! Please hurry! My friend's hurt badly!"

I didn't know if I was dreaming, but I heard voices, frantic and calm, loud and soft, near and far. Opening my eyes, I saw Vic looking toward the road above and yelling at someone. I wanted to talk, but my breath came in tiny gasps, each one bubbling blood.

Still cradling my head in his lap, Vic waved wildly at whoever stood on the road. The next thing I knew, strong hands gently lifted me onto a sled. *Is this real?* I wondered. Slow, steady movements pulled me up the steep ditch and onto the road above. Police and paramedics surrounded me. "Are you OK?" one asked, as he helped lift me into an ambulance. Unable to speak, I shook my head. Oh, how I wanted to scream for help and get whatever was wrong with me fixed.

Two paramedics, one on each side, began cutting off my shirt. They asked if I had drugs in my system. I didn't want to answer so I remained motionless. As soon as my shirt came off, they saw that both arms bore the bruises of countless nights slamming cocaine. The battlefield on my arms told the story.

Through the commotion came a voice I'll never forget. "I don't think we're going to make it." I wondered what he was talking about. Moments later it hit me. *They're talking about me!* At that point, had I been able, I'd have turned into the number one fan of the ambulance driver, cheering him on as if he were on the last lap of the Indy 500.

Then came, "We're going to give it a try!" The driver slammed the ambulance in gear, and I kept thinking, *Please, oh please. You have to make it. I can't die. I just can't die.* Next thing I knew, I was in a small emergency room. Nurses, doctors, and EMTs moved swiftly, putting me on a frame and then standing it almost upright. Only semi-conscious, I felt a doctor touch my chest and seemed to count my ribs. I can also remember his inserting a sharp, pointed surgical instrument (called a trocar) into a spot below my chest and under my arm. My lungs had collapsed, and without this procedure to drain the fluid, I'd simply have drowned in my own blood.

Almost immediately aides rushed me back to the ambulance and began the two-and-a-half hour drive to an intensive care unit in Calgary. The next few days were a blur. My injuries were so severe that doctors gave me a 50 percent chance of survival. After surgery, I floated in and out of consciousness. Pictures of my mom's and dad's faces flashed through my mind. Was I alive or in heaven? It didn't feel like heaven with constant feelings of anxiety, fear, and intense pain.

What made that annoying noise? Wrapped in tubes and wires, everything I saw and heard terrified me. A breathing tube stifled my cries for help—I couldn't talk. Wide-eyed I lay, having no idea what went on around me, only knowing that I felt helpless and alone. Then, as if on cue, I fell back asleep when the timely drip of morphine released me.

One day voices awoke me, and I saw the tearful, concerned faces of Mom and Dad hovering over me. Because the breathing apparatus prevented me from speaking, we used pencil and paper, and I found out exactly what was going on. I had lost the use of both lungs. One had collapsed but had been successfully re-inflated while the other had been punctured by broken ribs, and after a series of surgeries, two of the three lobes were gone. Although the surgery had been successful, infections had already caused complications twice, and both times the outlook had seemed grim.

My folks had organized prayer vigils and an anointing while my life hung in the balance. The thought of all these people praying for me brought mixed emotions—guilt and sadness for turning my back on such a group of loving Christians, but rage and anger that a loving God would let this happen to me. Completely unwilling to accept responsibility for my choices, I immediately began playing I-am-a-victim blame game. Poor me. Going from the life of a selfish junkie and then thrown directly into an environment of care and attention only fostered more selfishness and misery.

In my completely clouded and twisted mind, I began to reject even more the love and truth of God. I figured I was alive because I was lucky. Now that I lived on borrowed time, I should really start living life to the fullest. Satan had constructed and nurtured a totally deluded mind. Not even the miracle of life when I should have been dead fazed me.

One day an Adventist pastor visited me in my hospital room. I felt such hatred toward him that as he spoke about Christ, I wished I could spit on him. After the pastor left, I scolded my parents for trying to kick me when I was down. Are those Satan's delusions or what?

A month of hospital life left me skinny and hating the smells and sounds of medical care. After being released to my parents, we traveled back to their farm where I'd spent my childhood years. Occasionally they tried to talk about religion, but I'd shut it down immediately. I couldn't wait to get out and get high. After a few months, the opportunity came and, as planned, I didn't hesitate. I again smoked cigarettes and pot and drank whenever I could. What kind of a man could do drugs and alcohol after such a miraculous recovery and not see the handwriting on the wall?

Chapter 6

REHAB

Vancouver's Pacific National Exhibition (PNE) is the last stop on the Canadian west circuit of summer fairs. Kenny had disappeared the previous year, but I continued working for Sherri, his ex-wife. Rumors filled the air about Kenny's misfortune and fall from grace, but no one suspected that I, too, was a junkie. The summer had been long, and I was tired as the PNE wound down to the final days. I'd been using drugs heavily, staying up night after night, showing up to work gaunt and paranoid. The final weekend of a fair is always the moneymaker. With loads of people, last-minute buyers, and the expenses paid by midshow earnings, we referred to the last weekend as "gravy days."

Having been up for days, I sat alone in my hotel room getting high. The more coke I did, the more paranoid I became. I'd borrowed a stun gun from a friend because I had a room by myself and thought I could possibly be targeted for robbery. Things like this happen to pitchmen, especially in the final days of a fair. Thieves travel the shows, too, and know it's a cash business, but my fears were more fantasy than fact. During the night I began hearing voices and, peeping out the window, saw shadowy figures—all of which terrified me.

Could it be? I asked myself. *Has Kenny tracked me down in order to get some money?* Rumors swirled. He'd been spotted at the fairgrounds earlier that day. People said he was after Sherri and some money, but it was only hearsay. Nevertheless, as the night turned to morning, I became frantic—the voices and the shadows caused my paranoia to peak. Suddenly a knock on my door. I grabbed the stun gun, eased my way to the door, and peered out the peephole. Seeing a figure, I ripped the door open, stuck out the cracking, spitting gun, and jabbed at the person standing there. A shrill scream erupted as the terrified maid bolted away shrieking hysterically in a language I'd never heard. Slamming the door, I quickly locked and bolted it.

"Oh, my goodness. What did I just do?" I said over and over while pacing frenziedly.

Sweat poured down my face, and I knew I'd made a major mistake. The maid coming to service the room is met at the door by a raving lunatic who tried zapping her with a stun gun. But even in that psychopathic state, my addiction ruled calmly. I was rabid, but instead of flushing my bag of coke, I folded it up and stashed it under the mattress of my bed. Until then I'd paid no attention to time. Glancing at the clock, I felt a sickening feeling replace my hysteria—I was already late for work—something inexcusable in the business, especially on the busiest day.

Scrambling to get ready, I heard a knock on the door followed by a loud, commanding voice, "Open up! Vancouver police!" I froze motionless, the sound of my heart pounding in my head.

"Open up! Vancouver police!" barked from the other side.

"This cannot be happening," I whispered breathlessly as I slowly crept toward the door. Peering out the peephole, still not convinced that reality had finally arrived, I was stunned. Unlatching and unlocking my door, I moved back as the first wave of tense cops entered the room, guns drawn.

"Sit down on the bed, sir!" one ordered as they fanned out checking the closet and bathroom.

"OK. Where is it?" A burly looking older officer asked, as he holstered his gun,

"Where is what?" I replied.

"You know what I'm talking about. Where'd you put it?" he growled back.

Looking at him with deer-in-the-headlights eyes, I lied, "I have no idea what you're talking about." At this point I thought they might be referring to my stash hidden under the mattress. I'd never been arrested or even seen a gun drawn by a cop. I was petrified but possibly too strung out to really get what was going on. They continued to dismantle my room and suddenly a *thud* made every head turn. The stun gun hit the floor, and everyone seemed to freeze for a second.

"What's this?" the closest cop inquired holding it up like a dead fish.

"Oh! That's a stun gun; it's not illegal," I stated, as if I actually knew.

"Where's the real gun, Mr. Fleck? I'm tired of playing games with you! Where is it?" the burly one yelled.

"Real gun . . . you think I've got a real gun?" I questioned as things started to dawn on me. *They think I pointed a real gun at the maid,* I said to myself. *That's why they're so agitated.*

"Oh, wait just a minute here," I sputtered. "If you guys think I have a gun, you're all mistaken," I pleaded.

"So what did you point at the maid earlier? This thing?" he said pointing at the stun gun.

My silence confirmed their question. "Take him downtown. Run his name; see if he's got any warrants. . . ." The burly one continued giving orders as he escorted me out, down the stairs, and through the foyer.

I slunk through the lobby amid the stare of onlookers and into a waiting police car. Once downtown, embarrassed and scared, after having enough time to gather my wits, I concocted a story spun with a fictitious sighting of a crazed drug addicted ex-boss who was stalking me. At one point the officer stopped and asked if I was using drugs.

"Never!" I spat. "I'm a businessman." I don't know whether they bought it or not, but after an hour I was allowed to make a call.

"Sherri, I'm at the police department. I'll explain it all later. Just come get me." I hung up hoping my boss wouldn't be too upset to bail me out.

Some time later, Sherri arrived. Her eyes bore into mine. Then I followed her to the parking lot.

"Rick, you've really screwed up this time," she began as soon as we got into the company van.

"But Sherri, it was Kenny, and I . . ."

"Shut up and listen, Rick!" she shouted cutting off my babbling. "You're strung out. I've known for a while, and you need to clean up before you're any use to me or anyone! I love you like a son. That's why I called your dad an hour ago and told him what you've been up to."

"Whoa! Hold it, Sherri. What do you mean 'told him'? What did you tell him?"

"I told him you were strung out on drugs and needed help," she said with a choked voice, tears brimming in her eyes. "Rick, I've just been through years of drug abuse, putting up with Kenny. I know what's going on, and you need help." Dabbing her eyes with a tissue, she continued. "He said he'd be here tonight. He's flying into Vancouver and asked if you'd pick him up. Rick, it's over. You're done working for me or anyone in the business until you get help."

I felt betrayed and dejected. "How could you tell my dad?" I whined. "My parents don't need to know about this. I'll quit, Sherri. It's no problem," I lied. "Just let me work this final weekend, and then I'll get things fixed up," I begged knowing it was futile.

Arriving at the fairgrounds, Sherri parked the van, looked at me, and said, "What do you want to do now?" By midafternoon, the place was crawling with shoppers, but I knew I wouldn't see any of their money. My pitching days were done, at least for the time being. As soon as I knew for sure that Sherri wasn't going to weaken and I would not be working, I changed my attitude. Teary-eyed, I began a new manipulation. "Sherri, I need some money. I've got to go back, pack my things, and pay for the hotel."

She paused, thinking for a moment, and then unrolled a wad of cash, peeling me off a few hundred dollars. "The rest of your pay I'll send to your parents once you're home."

Smart lady, I thought to myself. So with very little cash and an appointment to pick up my dad, I waved down a cab and went back to the hotel. Walking into the same lobby I'd just been escorted through felt odd. Every bellman, desk clerk, and employee stared as if I had the plague. Yet something strange happened to me when I entered the hotel. A thought popped into my head. *I wonder if my coke is still there?* An anxious knot tightened in my stomach. Only an addict knows that feeling. Tunnel vision occurs, and the mind becomes obsessed with carrying out pleasure at any cost. Logic disappears, replaced by a fiendish desire with one objective, *satisfaction*—but that isn't the proper word because drugs never truly satisfy.

I walked to the front desk and was met by piercing stares and silence. "I'm here to pick up my clothes and pay my bill," I said, as if nothing had happened. Saying nothing, the manager slid my invoice across the counter. "I'm going to need to gather my things. May I have my room key?" I asked.

"Your things are already packed. Your bags are at the coat check," the manager's steely eyes stabbed back.

"Well, that was nice of you, but I won't be paying a dime until I see the room myself. I've got to make sure nothing was left behind," I said icily.

He paused. Knowing I had him, he grabbed a key and said, "Follow me." Nodding smugly I fell in behind him as we walked.

He opened the door and stood outside like a centurion. I went straight to the bed, lifted the mattress and, sure enough, my pleasure had remained hidden. I stashed the bag of coke in my pocket and walked out, not even bothering to look for left-behinds. I could not care less—tunnel vision told me it only would be minutes before that ringing sensation would put me back to that other dimension of chemical euphoria.

Paying quickly, I strolled to my car, threw in the luggage, and bee-lined to the nearest gas station, where I locked myself in the public restroom and, undisturbed, carried out the ritual of getting high. I spent the remainder of that afternoon hopscotching from station to station on my way to the airport, getting high in each restroom. Evening came, and in a drugged haze I arrived at the airport, chain-smoking and out of cocaine. Nervously, I waited, pacing by the gate where my father would arrive, half of me trying to focus on reality, the other half brainstorming how I could go find some more coke.

Fortunately, my dad soon appeared in the crowd. Like the prodigal son, I burst into tears as I reached out to receive the most loving hug I could ever remember. The strength of his arms and Christlike forgiveness in his eyes melted my anxiety and chased the fiendlike demons away. We stood embraced for a time, both sobbing, without saying any other words except "I love you. I love you." We walked to my car, got in, and left Vancouver with all its madness behind.

A day later we arrived in Calgary and pulled into a hotel where my mother was waiting. I was unsure of what they had planned, but it soon became evident they weren't letting me talk my way out of this situation. They contacted a counselor who came over to evaluate me. Still trying to avoid any huge changes, I desperately attempted to manipulate and lie my way out, claiming I'd just started and wasn't a real addict. Listening intently, jotting down notes, the counselor seemed to be buying my pitch, or at least that's what I thought.

With the interview completed, she called my parents to come into the room and sit down. Surveying the scene, I thought it strange—my mom and dad, a therapist, and me sitting in a hotel together deciding my future. Only a few days before I was working and living my life. Now everything had changed. *How long will it be until I start work again?* I wondered to myself. *A week, maybe two . . . no big deal. I'll fake it. They'll lay off. I'll be back to normal before long.*

"OK, Rick," the voice of the counselor stopped my daydream. "You and your family have some hard choices to make."

I shrugged, thinking she was being a little overdramatic.

"Well, what have you got?" I joked trying to lighten the mood. Nobody smiled.

"Rick, you've got a severe addiction, a terminal disease, and if left untreated, it will kill you. It can't be cured, but it can be maintained with therapy and a lot of work. Your choices are simple: Continue without treatment and you'll die. Get help and you could possibly live, although you'll be an addict the rest of your life. I'm going to let you and your folks decide. Here's my card. Flights leave for Long Beach daily. . . ."

Her voice trailed off into thin air. "Death, addiction, treatment? Long Beach? You mean California? You're crazy!"

"Mom and Dad, you've got to believe me. This woman is nuts. I'm no addict! Hey, I'll take a few weeks, kick it with you guys on the farm, and I'll be fine."

My words fell on deaf ears. Their jaws were set and emotions resigned to the fact that I was not OK—in fact, I was seriously ill. I argued, but to no avail, and by that evening we were calling to reserve a flight.

*   *   *   *   *

The Long Beach Memorial Medical Center's drug treatment program in Southern California was only a day away, but I wasn't ready to relinquish my addiction yet. An old friend picked me up at the airport and, with only a few words, I convinced him I could check in to the drug rehab the next day. Hesitantly he agreed, having been asked by my parents to take me straight to the hospital. We chatted and caught up on things, but my mind was only half-attentive. The old knot was forming in my chest—the anxious feeling of knowing I could find drugs if I manipulated him properly.

After all, I'm going to rehab. I deserve a little treat before I give it up. Don't I? I reasoned to myself.

We reached his place and after some more catching up and dinner, he said, "I've got school tomorrow, so I should crash. Feel free to make yourself at home." With that he retired to his room, but I stayed up chain-smoking on his balcony while scheming how to get high.

The next morning he was off to school. I borrowed his car, picked up some beer at the corner store, and cruised the local strip. Within a couple hours I'd located and purchased some drugs. Just like that I was back into my addiction. It didn't matter where I was. It ruled supreme; no geographic changes were going to silence the fiend inside me. When my buddy returned home, he looked at me in disgust, more in sympathy than anger, and said, "Get your stuff. I'm taking you to Long Beach."

"No, Brother, I can go tomorrow," I begged.

"Nope, we're going now." The finality in his voice silenced me. Just before we left, the phone rang. A worried and anxious voice spoke, "Rick, what are you doing?" My mom's quivering voice pleaded, "The hospital called and said you didn't make it. Please, son, please go."

"OK, Mom. OK, I'm going." I hung up.

Why can't I just be left alone? I thought to myself, not realizing that drugs controlled every aspect of my deceitful life. Within a couple of hours I stood in the lobby of the hospital not knowing what to expect but thinking it was going to be a cushy country-club-like experience, enabling me to get sober. I strolled in, golf clubs over one shoulder, suit bag over the other, pulling a suitcase on wheels, looking as if I were ready for a vacation. I could've sworn I saw several smirks and heard muffled laughter coming from the attendants.

"Hi, I'm Rick Fleck. I'm here from Canada for the rehab," I said.

The nurse looked past me at my belongings and smiled. Nodding to a scrub-clad employee to my left, she said, "Will you find a place for Mr. Fleck's belongings?"

When the helper reached for my things, I resisted. "Hold on. I'm going to need some things to wear," I objected.

"No, Mr. Fleck. You won't need any of that for quite some time. This isn't Club Med—it's a hospital. Now give the attendant your things and fill out this questionnaire." She smiled and handed me a clipboard with a page full of questions. Angry, I glared at her, then at the attendant, as my belongings disappeared down the sterile hallway.

After I had filled out the questionnaire, the attendant escorted me to a two-bed hospital room and asked me to supply a urine sample. When the door closed, the smells, the crisp bedding, the silence all closed in at once. I buried my face in the unfriendly blanket and sobbed like a spoiled brat.

"What's going on?" I cried out loud. "I'm no drug addict. This is crazy. I shouldn't be here!" My mind churned out previously used rationalizations.

"Why are all these people doing this to me? What's wrong with them?" I tried to think logically, something impossible to do with the mind of a strung-out junkie, the only mind I had left. I felt abandoned, alone, and forgotten—but the reality was exactly the opposite. My family and friends had sacrificed much and only wanted the old Rick back. It was all for my own good, but I couldn't see it. At that moment I hated everyone.

The sound of the door wrested me from my thoughts. The same admitting nurse entered with the same clipboard and questionnaire.

"OK, Mr. Fleck. By the looks of your urine analysis, we'll need to redo the questionnaire from the beginning. I might add that everyone working in this rehab is a recovering addict, so nothing you're about to say is anything new. We've all sat in your seat at some time. Your lies and manipulation stop here. Am I clear?"

"Um . . . uh, OK. But, I . . . um." Looking into her eyes, I knew she wasn't about to buy any spiel from me, so I conceded.

"OK, Mr. Fleck, question one: When was the last time you used? You said a week ago, but your urine shows you're legally drunk now, among other things." She stood patiently waiting for my response. I tried giving her a look of disbelief, but it was futile. "You also have cocaine, pot, and methamphetamine in your system. Care to comment?" she tapped her pen on the clipboard.

I knew she couldn't be fooled, so I spilled my guts. Like a dam breaking, my emotions drained out onto a set of sympathetic ears. As soon as she saw me break, her attitude softened, allowing me to get started on the road to recovery. Honesty—step one. With the questionnaire properly filled out, she sat and explained what I could expect in the next few days.

This stage was detox—minimum of forty-eight hours—then I'd be evaluated and, depending on my condition, moved to the regular rooms where rehab would begin.

Forty-eight hours. I pondered her words. *That's a long time to sit in a bed with nothing to do. I don't think I can make it.* But before long, I passed out, the weight of the world lifted, and I slept for a day. This rehab specialized in cocaine addiction—it was also covered by my parents' insurance. Minimum of thirty days, depending on the progress, and all done in a hospital setting. The month inched by; never had time passed so slowly. Used to the fast pace of sales and travel, I found inactivity a shock all by itself, never mind the gnawing knot of addiction set deep in my chest. But amazingly, as the days crawled by, clarity began to peek through. The group therapy and treatment made sense, and I was sober—a foreign but pleasant feeling. The fourth week was family week, when the closest relatives get reacquainted with the sober addict. Nervously, I waited till I saw my family walk through the hospital door. Then I smothered them with hugs and soaked them with tears.

We decided that I would move into a halfway house after the thirty days of rehab ended. We found one in Newport Beach on the boardwalk that winds its way along the beach. I'd never lived in any place so beautiful and serene where I could enjoy early morning walks on the beach, watch the fog roll out, smell salt air, and hear waves crash on the shore.

I wanted to digest it all and put it in a safe place. I couldn't remember ever feeling so alive and happy. The happiness was innocent and pure, and I wanted to keep it forever. I couldn't remember feeling so alive and content. This happiness made the contrast between my old and new lifestyle vast and undeniable.

Who would want to go back to being a junkie? I asked myself many times during those walks. *Only an idiot would ever screw up this feeling.*

Little did I know what was lurking just below the surface of this newfound peace.

Chapter 7

RELAPSE

About a month after leaving the hospital while living at the Newport Beach halfway house, a friend of a friend who'd heard I was in the area contacted me. He needed a chamois pitchman for a car show in Long Beach.

After talking to my counselor, we decided it would be OK as long as I still attended an Alcoholics Anonymous (AA) meeting in the morning, a requirement of all in the halfway house. A three-day weekend show isn't a big money spot, but potentially I could make a few bucks.

I met Paul, a promoter about my age, who said he'd heard I was good when sober. "I hope you plan on staying sober. I'll give you a chance. Don't screw it up." He slapped me on the shoulder as I promised to do my best. The first day I doubled his figures from the previous year. I felt *so* alive, every sense tuned, my mind sharp—and people were spending money. By the end of the weekend, Paul's smile revealed his approval; he'd never grossed so much at this car-show event. He gave me a thousand dollars, and with no drugs or booze to buy, the money didn't dwindle.

A couple weekends later, Paul called and asked if I'd work a home show at Dodgers' Stadium. Of course I jumped at the chance, and another thousand dollars fell into my lap. Driving home one night it all dawned on me. It wasn't luck. It wasn't chance. I was sober, and I could really sell even without the drugs. A thought crossed my mind that hadn't been there in many years. *Is the success from God?* AA talks about a Higher Power, which I just assumed to be God. Having been raised a Seventh-day Adventist, I didn't find *God* a foreign word. Actually, in honest, introspective moments, I admitted that God may have had a hand in saving my life in that car accident. Still unsure about the "God thing," I was sure of one thing—life seemed better each day. Opportunities fell into my lap, and I made the most of them.

After about three months at the halfway house, I received a phone call. A familiar voice pumped with enthusiasm rang through the lines. "Rick, it's Vic. How in the world are ya?" I couldn't believe it. My friend with whom I experienced that horrible car wreck was on the other end. I'd heard he went to Florida and had started a pitch company, working the swap meets and flea markets. "Hey, there, Buddy. Long time, no hear!"

I laughed. "So what are you doing?" I asked.

"Well, Brother," he began, "I started a little business down here and need a solid partner I can trust—you know of anyone?" My heart started pounding as we jabbered back and forth.

"Hey, I'm sober, too," he continued. "Quit everything after I heard what happened to you. So, how about it? Wanna come down?"

"Let me see," I responded. "I've got to talk to a few people before I make a decision. I'll get back to you." With our goodbyes said, I hung up—almost vibrating with excitement about yet another huge opportunity.

"Partnership in my own pitch company. That's a dream come true." The words fell like bombs on the ears of my folks as I explained Vic's offer on the phone. They remembered that only a couple years earlier, Vic and I had a narrow escape from being killed in a car wreck caused by drugs and lack of sleep. I knew they weren't feeling pleased, but I pressed on. "I'm sober now. So is Vic. It'll be good. We can go to AA meetings in Florida. I'll be OK."

Trying to convince them, I spoke what I thought was truth. So young in sobriety, I didn't realize I had much to learn. I packed my car, and two days later I drove into Ft. Lauderdale, Florida. The balmy humid ocean air filled my nostrils. I had a sense of accomplishment, and an air of ego-centered pride consumed me. Vic and I discussed the deal, and I bought in, now a partner in my own business. It wasn't long until a new product came our way, Didi Seven®, a fantastic new stain remover from Germany. The distributors from Canada had asked us to handle their United States demo sales.

I couldn't believe our luck. We started pitching it all over the country, hiring more and more agents. Our business took off. We booked a show in New York City called the International Business Services. I decided to go myself and contacted a friend I'd met at rehab who now lived in New York City. Having never been there before, I figured he would be perfect to work with and for showing me around.

He jumped at the chance. We met, and the first thing I asked him was, "Are you still sober?"

He paused, looked down, and then back at me.

"Scott, are you sober?" I said again with a little more emphasis on *sober*.

He sighed and shook his head. "No, Rick, that's something I've been meaning to tell you."

"It's been only six months. What happened?"

"Well, I don't know. Man, I was doing good, then . . ." he hung his head. "It just happened, Brother. I can't explain it. I feel terrible but now that you're here, maybe I'll be able to clean up."

"I hope so, Scott. We need to be clean, or we've lost everything we've struggled for." I tried encouraging him but could see the disappointment in his eyes. We set up the show and started Friday morning. Ten thousand dollars' worth of Didi Seven sat in our booth. Having never worked this show before, I figured that should be enough. The doors opened, and more people than I ever could have imagined spilled through the hallways. Instantly the aisles were packed. I started my first pitch and something strange happened. A sea of faces stopped and, like shavings to a magnet, locked on to my voice, moving, pushing, and shoving to see the demonstration. I knew Didi Seven had been on television but didn't know that New York City had been the main advertised area.

These people were frenzied—yelling, elbowing, jerking their purses open to find their wallets, calling, "How much is it? How much is the Didi Seven?"

Scott scrambled into action assuming the cashier's role. We took money nonstop, pausing only for a splash of soda to wet my lips.

I pitched like a mad man. At about 3:00 P.M. Scott tugged on my leg. "Not now, Scott, I'm busy," I snapped.

"That's it, Rick, it's gone. It's all gone," Scott replied.

"Huh? What's gone?" I said in disbelief.

"The stuff, man. The cleaning stuff. It's all gone," Scott said again. I looked around, seeing only empty boxes. The booth looked like a disaster area—demo ink, dyes, water, and cleanser were splashed everywhere. And he was right. It was *all* gone. Ten thousand dollars' worth in just a few hours. I could not believe my eyes when Scott opened a brown bag displaying the loot.

"Wow! This is really living!" I yelled out loud. Scott stood in amazement. "So how'd you like the pitch business so far, Scott?" I laughed, eyes dancing with dollar signs. "Here's a few hundred. Is that cool for the day?"

He sputtered, smiled, and then gave me a hug. "Thanks, Rick. I really need the money."

I felt like a big shot, and pride welled up inside. Full of myself, I told Scott to clean things up while I found a phone and called Vic in Florida. After blowing Vic's mind with the unexpected news and organizing a shipment via air to arrive Saturday afternoon, I moseyed back to the booth. "So, Buddy, what do you say I take you out to dinner?" I asked like a big shot.

"Well, sure, if you want to. I could eat," Scott agreed.

"Where to? Where's a nice spot we can relax and enjoy ourselves?"

"Let me think. How about Mr. Chow's, an upscale Chinese restaurant in the heart of the city?" he suggested.

"Lead the way, my friend." Once out of the convention center, we were met with an icy cold breeze. Usually packed with yellow taxis, the street was unusually quiet. For this time of night, only a few limos sat purring beside the curb.

"How about a limo, Scott? I think we've earned it." He nodded, grinning from ear to ear. We hopped in the warm, luxurious stretch limo, taking in the unmistakable ambiance of richness—leather seats, mirrors, plush carpeting, a mini bar, phone, and all the extras.

"Where to, Gentlemen?" the polite driver asked in a way that made me feel like I owned the city. With my head swollen with pride, I said "Mr. Chows!" like I was somebody special. On the way, Scott had an idea. Eyeing the car phone, he suggested we call a couple girls. Not recognizing the path I'd already stepped on to, I said, "Sure, great idea."

We arrived at the restaurant, sat down, and soon two women in their twenties entered. Waving, they made their way over and after intros sat down. The waiter appeared with a menu and asked for our drink orders. The first red flag exposed itself in my subconscious.

"Drinks? I don't drink." I almost said out loud.

I watched the girls order, then Scott. He looked at me with a questioning stare that said without words, "Should you have one?" A weird silent moment happened that I'll never forget.

The past few hours of fantasy had blurred my reality. The events of the day masked the truth. I was still an addict. The money, city lights, limo, women, and fancy restaurant fed my addiction.

Time stood still. Then, from somewhere, I heard a voice saying, "Let's have champagne." It was mine. That night was the six-month anniversary or "birthday" of my first sober day. Instead of celebrating it in an AA meeting, I disgraced it by drinking.

The rest of the night remains a blur. More limos, more booze, and ultimately, before the sun came up, I had a needle once again chasing me into another dimension. *What have I done? What have I done?* I sat alone in my hotel room, sobbing uncontrollably. I felt like killing myself. *Why, why, why?* I asked myself over and over, burying my head in my pillows unable to sleep. I had failed, I had relapsed. Sitting in AA meetings, listening to people relive their failures hadn't prepared me for this. So many people supported and trusted me. Now I had let them all down. I was left with two choices: honesty and dishonesty—dishonesty came naturally now, so it wasn't a hard decision.

I told Scott to keep this little episode between us. He agreed. So I once again began living a lie. Nobody knew. I still could be the golden boy who conquered drug addiction and was doing well.

Our business continued to boom. Vic and I made a decision to move. Demographically, Connecticut was better for sales, so we decided to set up shop there—easy access to millions of people and tons of shows. Throughout the next year, I stayed clean when at the office or around town. Danbury, Connecticut, was small enough to not have an area secret enough for me to find drugs. I felt safe there going to work and coming home. But every so often a show would come up in another state that we didn't have an available agent to cover. I'd raise my hand and volunteer, knowing exactly what was in store. As soon as I got on the plane bound for wherever, I'd "order up," beginning a weekend of seventy-two hours of partying. Just me, all alone, a closet junkie, ferreting out the drugs that accompany seedy bars lining dark streets. Then, as if nothing had happened, I'd be at the office Monday morning talking about the weekend's sales, all the while nursing bruised arms under long-sleeved shirts, every time feeling a little less guilty and a little more cunning. However, our business began to decline. Didi Seven, the amazing cleaner, was getting played out, and inexperience and mismanagement soon took its toll. Vic and I parted, each blaming the other and abandoning the outstanding debts. With two cars loaded, my girlfriend, Misty, and I headed for the West Coast.

Once back in California, a familiar peace came over me. Memories of sobriety flooded my mind. I wondered, as I drank a beer, how many of my rehab acquaintances actually had remained sober.

Temecula is nestled in the warm Southern California desert. Palm trees surround oasis-style golf courses. Rolling hills and hidden lakes treat the eyes. Surveying the landscape, I fell in love with the area. Two hours from Los Angeles and about the same from San Diego, I thought it was a perfect location. I quickly set up a new company and began booking shows. Finally my own boss with no bickering partner, I could take the failed experience of Didi Seven and build my own empire.

Chapter 8

SORCERY
OF GREED

During this time I met Greg, a fellow pitchman as wide as he was tall and all muscle from spending hours in the gym and thousands of dollars on steroids. He hit me up one day about possibly doing some business. Since I now lived in Southern California with Mexico only a couple of hours away, we soon came to an agreement that when the summer fair season closed, we'd do a little extra marketing.

Always open to making money, I was all ears when he disclosed his steroid racket. Like a shark to chum, I squirmed when he told me how much money he made selling steroids. We parted, but a couple of months later, after the fair season closed, I called him. He faxed a list of top-selling steroids to look for, we discussed the financial side briefly, and off I went to Mexico. Misty and I packed some things, hopped in the car, and three hours later were cruising the streets of Tijuana. Having never looked for drugs in Mexico before, I felt quite nervous but started asking in pharmacies for steroids. To my surprise, none of the stores seemed to have the slightest idea what I wanted. Store after store, the clerks just looked at me as if I had a tail.

Becoming aggravated and suspecting they had the stuff but were afraid to sell, I decided to go farther south. We went to the airport, parked the car, and walked into the terminal. My jaw was set—I would find steroids come what may. I bought tickets to Cabo San Lucas, located on the tip of Baja, California, on the Gulf of Mexico. Arriving a couple hours later, I thought, *Now what?* as I looked around the poverty-stricken little town. After checking into a hotel, I set out to land that elusive catch. At the first pharmacy, I asked for a couple of the drugs on my list and, to my surprise, the answer was instant. With a courteous smile the lady pulled out a couple of boxes and laid them on the counter. *Wow,* I thought. *This is the jackpot.* Only a half block from my hotel I'd hit pay dirt.

But when I asked her about prices, we soon bogged down because she didn't speak English, and I didn't want to solicit a translator for this transaction. Sensing this, she picked up a phone, motioned for me to stay, and walked away. Soon a jeep pulled up beside the little store, and out jumped a large Mexican wearing an even larger cowboy hat. Bursting into the store, he greeted me with a smile and open hand. Motioning me to follow, he led me into a small storeroom with a makeshift desk and a cooler full of cold drinks. After dismissing his overanxious wife, Juan began in almost flawless English. "You want to buy steroids? I have steroids."

For the next hour we haggled back and forth on prices. We came to an agreement, shook hands, and off I went to the pool at the hotel to let Misty know of our good fortune. She listened and seemed interested, but I could see apprehension in her eyes. A few days later Juan called, and I returned to the little store. His jeep had boxes piled up in the back covered with a large sheet. I looked at the boxes just knowing they couldn't all be mine. When I entered the store, there stood Juan, sweat pouring down his face, sipping a soda and looking as if he'd just lassoed a longhorn steer. "There's your *medicina*," he huffed. "Now let's get the *dinero*." I smiled, sat down, and began counting out four thousand dollars, all the time wondering how I could get all that stuff back to the States.

After settling the finances, we took the drugs to my room and stacked them against the wall. Sitting on the bed staring at all the boxes, I wondered if I'd just made a serious mistake. Mexico is very corrupt, and the law and those who break it are often one and the same. Juan had told me that his cousin was a *federali,* which is like a sheriff in the U.S.—only with more authority. I started thinking how easy it would be for Juan to call his cousin, raid my hotel, take the drugs, and put me in a hole face-down. My fears weren't unreasonable because such a scenario often happens in Mexico. As soon as I could rent a car, we packed up and moved to a different hotel so Juan wouldn't know our whereabouts. That night I slept a little better, although every time I'd look at those boxes, a wave of anxiety swept over me.

Misty and I vacationed in Cabo for another few days before heading home. But first, I needed to camouflage the cargo. At a local tourist shop, I purchased a couple of giant suitcases and two duffel bags. We spent the next day repacking the preloaded syringes, ampoules, and bottles of illegal steroids. The nine boxes soon shrank into the four touristy-looking travel bags I'd bought. Then we checked out of the hotel and drove to the airport.

Mexico airport security is weak at best, but unlike United States security, it's very unpredictable. When boarding a domestic flight in Cabo San Lucas, a traveler goes through two steps. First is the metal detection. Next, the traveler must follow a yellow line leading to what looks like a traffic light, which flashes red or green when each person advances. To the left is the boarding area. To the right is an inspection area, where officers search the passenger's luggage. As I surveyed the situation, I could not figure out why some passengers got the green light and some the red. Feeling prickly paranoia, I backtracked to the car, got in, and sat down. After coming this far, I was chickening out.

I weighed the pros and cons, but soon greed for profit and fast cash took over. I might be crazy, but I'm not stupid, so I drove back to the bus depot. Picking up some big boxes marked "glassware," I unloaded all the drugs into margarita-glass shipping boxes, put them on the bus, and sent them on their way to Tijuana. What a genius I thought I was! Now we could return home and in a few days drive back to Tijuana and pick up the boxes at the bus depot.

A few days later I asked my Spanish-speaking neighbor to call, and he confirmed that my cargo was in. So off we went the following Sunday, knowing that around 2:00 P.M. the line at the border would be filled with tourists coming home from the weekend. After picking up the boxes, we put the contents back into suitcases, bought a couple sombreros, some pottery, and a poncho, hoping to look like every other American after a weekend of fun in Mexico. U.S. border patrol agents tend to search vehicles according to a profile, and we hoped to avoid suspicion.

Sure enough, the lines to the border were miles long as people inched their way home. With each foot nearer to the custom's checkpoint, I became more fidgety and anxious. Misty asked whether I was OK. I wasn't. Fear, paranoia, and anxiety were overwhelming me. Finally, she could no longer take the stress and told me to let her drive. I couldn't believe it. She wasn't in favor of this drug dealing, but she appeared as calm as could be. I jumped at the offer, my cowardice and greed sacrificing her just that quickly.

As we approached the border, I pretended to be asleep, and she performed flawlessly. When the inspector waved us through, I felt an instant rush of victory, thanking her, God, and everyone else. I'd never felt this feeling before—elation, excitement, and bravado. I acted as if I'd just won the lottery.

Misty, on the other hand, wasn't so excited. She calmly said, "Rick, if you ever do this again, count me out; and, furthermore, if you do it again, I'll leave you!" Her words went in one ear and out the other. In my selfish, greedy mind, her safety wasn't even an issue; it was all about the money and me.

I sent the cargo to Bellingham, Washington, the next day and received twelve thousand dollars. Wow! Was this the life or what?

Spend four thousand dollars, go to Mexico, lie around the pool for ten days, come home, and receive twelve thousand dollars for the trip. All I could see were dollar signs, and soon, forgetting about the fear and danger, I began secretly planning my next trip to Cabo, with or without Misty. The seeds planted so long before had sprouted, and now a large tree drove its roots into my soul, bearing the fruits of greed that soon choked all logic and morality.

Later that year I met Ed, a person close to Misty's family. An easy-going guy, he seemed never to have a care. Always happy, never in a rush, he stayed at our house for a while. One day I asked Misty what he did for a living. She shrugged and said, "Sells pot." I was shocked. He didn't look like a drug dealer. He was well kept, polite, never out late at night, didn't drink—but he did always have a little pot to smoke. Having now become an everyday pot smoker myself, I was impressed by the quality of his pot. He'd always give me a bit, and I thought this was his way of thanking me for letting him stay at our house off and on.

One day when I approached him about possibly doing a little business, he never batted an eye; he seemed to know I'd bite at the bait of easy money. We sat on my sofa, and after discussing business and prices, I said, "When do we get started?" He disappeared for a minute and soon returned with a bag of pot as big as any I'd seen. "Here's a pound," he said, "worth a thousand dollars, but you can have it for four hundred dollars. Don't bother paying me until you've sold it."

Just like that I had a pound of pot and an invitation to sell at my leisure, costing me nothing in advance. I'd already done some checking in the local area and knew I had a great opportunity and a great price. It took only a couple days to sell that pound, and I asked for more. After a few weeks, Ed said he'd be out of town for a while but would leave me ten pounds to work with until he returned. Again I had to smile—a proud, greedy smile of a drug dealer.

When he returned, I had a pile of cash waiting for him. We exchanged stories, but he soon had my full attention as he told me about a sweet several-hundred-pound deal he'd turned over in Colorado. Then he changed gears and asked for a favor. I jumped at the chance saying, "Sure!"

"Look, Rick," he began. "I'm meeting a couple of guys in San Diego and picking up a pretty good issue, but I need a ride. Can you give me a hand?"

Feeling like a big shot, I said, "No problem."

"Rick, I don't expect you to do this for free, so in exchange for the favor, I'll introduce you to my connection; that way you won't have to wait for me when this is gone. He smiled. "Plus, your price will be cheaper and any quantity you need will always be available."

What a deal! I was pumped. This sounded like a win-win situation. From Temecula, it was a straight shot down Interstate 15 to San Diego. The four-lane highway usually had little traffic but had one minor hiccup, a border-patrol checkpoint. I'd been through it many, many times. At that time it was usually open only a couple days a week, and I'd never been stopped. Typically, the officials would slow cars, glance inside, and wave them through. Trucks were sometimes stopped and searched for illegal aliens, but normally it was just a smile and a nod for passenger cars.

One evening a few days later, we headed south. A warm breeze caressed the hills covered with avocado orchards. With soft tunes playing in the car stereo, I felt as if I hadn't a care until Ed directed me to turn off the interstate and into a very dark and sinister-looking neighborhood in San Diego. Small rundown houses lined the streets; broken-down vehicles littered the driveways. We crept through the unlit streets until Ed motioned me to pull into a driveway. Killing the motor, I sat for a moment, goose bumps crawling on my skin, before opening the door. Two men appeared out of the shadows, said something in Spanish, and motioned us into the side door of a windowless garage.

In the inky darkness feebly illuminated only by a small clip-on lamp attached to a sawhorse, I saw ghostly silhouettes bouncing off the wall and a large black tarp obviously covering something big.

All sorts of ghoulish thoughts ran through my mind. *Here we are in a garage with at least two drug smugglers. No telling who or what else is in the adjoining house. Ed, coming to make a big purchase of drugs, obviously carries a large amount of cash, and I am standing in front of a large plastic tarp that could easily be used to protect the concrete of the mess involved with disposing of two bodies.* I wanted out, but with that option no longer available, I feared leaving as much as staying. I stood trembling, trying to look calm but knowing I was anything but.

One man pulled back the tarp, and the weak light of the single bulb lay the biggest pile of green marijuana I'd ever seen. The smell of the buds instantly filled the air, and everyone seemed to relax a bit—at least I did. But the situation was still dangerous. They'd not seen Ed's money yet, and that would be the moment of truth or die. Ed picked and poked at the buds, sniffing, rolling, and examining it like a farmer would his prize alfalfa. After what seemed forever, he nodded and opened his jacket, revealing a bulging fanny pack. The tension increased as he pulled out stacks of carefully counted and wrapped bills.

A new sound! What is it? I froze with new panic. *A door opening. Oh no, God,* I prayed to myself. Light streamed in the sliver of open door as two more silhouettes emerged from a side room.

My heart once again pounded. *This is it,* I thought silently. Trembling and trying hard not to show it, I stood silently, waiting. The two carried a duffle bag and set it on the floor by the pot. It made a clanking sound as it hit the ground. *Metal? Oh great,* I waited for the guns and butcher knives to appear. But to my relief, they produced a scale and began piling on the weed, weighing out pound after pound. Ed counted the pounds as his counterpart thumbed through the stacks of money. Then a couple of Hefty® Cinch Sak® garbage bags appeared, and we stuffed in the weighed contents.

With the giant bags filled, the garage door opened, Ed grabbed the sacks, and I hurried to open the trunk of my car. He put them on top of my golf clubs and a stack of Create.A.Curtains. What lay in the trunk summed up my life: Create.A.Curtain, my legitimate business; golf, my passion; and drugs, my secret, dark side. *Why do I bother with drugs while maintaining a thriving legitimate business?* I asked myself. That's the insanity; that's the evil of greed and addiction.

I sped out of the seedy neighborhood and onto the interstate heading home. With music playing, I relaxed enough for the saliva to return, enabling me to once again swallow and speak. "That was exciting," I said to Ed. *Almost too exciting,* I thought to myself. But I had done it—once again tempting disaster and walking away untouched. After about an hour, just outside of Escondido, I noticed a troubling sight: the lights of the border-patrol checkpoint blazing and patrolmen checking vehicles. My saliva once again dried up. "What is going on?" I wondered out loud.

Ed shrugged and maintained his usual unflappable composure.

"I've never seen the checkpoint open at midnight," I mused. As we neared, I could make out a row of trucks idling on the far right lane, waiting to be searched, but officers waved other cars through as usual. I calmed for a moment weighing the odds of being checked. I'd never been checked, and with blond hair, a tank top, and late model car, I didn't think I would. We slowed to a crawl as the official motioned for me to roll down my window and stop. This was a first; I'd never been stopped before.

"Where are you going?" he asked.

"Home," I replied.

"Where do you live?"

"Temecula," I stammered.

"Where were you today?" I felt as if he knew everything about me and expected to catch me lying.

"We went to play golf in San Diego," I replied.

He took one more look at Ed and me and motioned us forward but not to continue down the interstate. He walked in front of my car, directing me to pull into the inspection area. As if guiding a plane to a standstill on the tarmac, he motioned for us to cut the engine under a bank of huge halogen lights, which seemed to penetrate through the very roof of my car. He ordered us out and advised me of my rights.

"Is this your car?"

"Yes."

"Anything in the car such as drugs, money, guns, or anything illegal will be considered yours. Do you understand?"

"Yes," I said quietly.

"Get out of the car."

I obeyed.

"Open the trunk," he ordered. *This is it,* I thought. *He knows; he's been tipped off. Should I run? Spill my guts?* A myriad of options raced through my mind as I turned the key to the trunk lock. Lifting it, I looked away and stood back a few feet with Ed, whose demeanor had not changed. I could see the two giant bags with the telltale points of marijuana stems poking through the sides. But in addition to the large bags was another giveaway— from ten feet away I could plainly smell the sweet aroma of marijuana. The officer looked into the trunk and then motioned to an adjacent trailer.

Seconds later a tan German shepherd dog appeared with his handler. The dog's eager yips signaled to his trainer that he was ready to bury me. At this moment I found myself praying to a Friend I'd once known and loved. I don't know how long I'd been praying; perhaps I started subconsciously when we first were pulled over. I now deeply conversed with the only One left,

Oh God, oh God, please don't let this happen. If You get me out of this, I'll never do it again. Sound familiar?

The dog made a beeline straight for the open trunk, hopped up, and stuck his nose in the middle of a hundred thousand dollars' worth of prime marijuana. I held my breath. It all seemed to be happening in slow motion. Not wanting to look up, I heard the dog jump down and begin circling the car. I stole a peek as he hopped onto the backseat, then the front, and back around to the front tire on the passenger side. He seemed very interested in that tire for some reason, and a second later I knew why, as he moved a foot forward and up and promptly began relieving himself. The trainer yanked his collar, abruptly interrupting what was to me the most joyful sight I'd ever seen. The first officer stepped forward, handed me the keys, and said, "You're free to go."

I closed the trunk, hiding what could've landed me many years in prison. I was trembling as I slid behind the wheel, closed the door, and stared in my mirrors, waiting for the big bust, but none came.

For the next few miles, Ed and I said nothing. I continued to watch the mirror thinking it was all a setup, thinking any minute I'd see helicopters and hear sirens, but nothing happened. Eventually, I pulled into my driveway, shut off the engine, and walked into the house. Slumping on the couch, I began to relax, with the night's activities playing over and over again until I fell asleep.

The next day I could think only of how lucky I had been. I felt almost invincible; nobody could catch me. I didn't recall my prayers to God until sometime later when He once again became real to me. God had given me opportunities to see His hand in my life. He had answered my foxhole prayers and delivered me from disaster time and again. But my greed and addiction would soon cause Jesus to lift His sheltering hand and let me reap what I had sown.

Chapter 9

OUT OF
CONTROL

In the pitch business hierarchy, the pitchman can advance to promoter and then to manufacturer. Getting to the top takes drive and willingness to take risks. As a pitchman I always knew that even if one week the biggest show failed due to snow or rain, I could go to the dinkiest flea market the following week and make a killing. This knowledge took the fear from risking the costs of a big show and fed the insanity of feeling invincible.

Pitchmen earn 25 percent of gross sales and receive cash every night—no checks, no income tax or deductions, no questions— a roll of bills every working day.

The promoter assumes all financial responsibility for an event: He buys the merchandise, estimates the sales, and pays for booth rental and shipping costs. He takes the risks, but if the show is a bonanza, he reaps the riches. A promoter also can work his own booth, and many do, making that much more money. When I started promoting, I'd see a hot item, look for the wholesaler (often secretly ripping off address labels from discarded boxes in the back of someone's booth), and make a call.

The manufacturer, at the top of the heap, discovers an undeveloped product or knocks off a look-alike and piggybacks on the original's advertisement and fame. Manufacturers overseas

67

are masters of the knockoff, but their timing is usually a bit late because of the time it takes to make a knockoff, ship it, and distribute it. If I found a popular item, manufactured it, and distributed it before the masses of containers arrived from China and Taiwan, I could make a killing.

Not everyone had the funds or guts to put everything on the line, but I lacked neither, possibly because I had no real respect for money and knew how easily it could come and go. The business is finicky—one minute a product is hot; the next minute people don't want it even if it is given to them for free. So a manufacturer must be doubly on his toes, or he'll have a warehouse full of product he can't even give away.

After ten years in the business, I finally got my big break. New York is the hub of gadgets and new items, a crossroads between manufacturers, promoters, and pitchmen. One winter at a show in Manhattan, the same show where years before I'd first used crack, I came out of the stalls, clearing my burning throat and running nose, and was stunned to see a guy in a small ten-foot booth attracting a huge crowd. At the end of the day, crowds were thinning, but this guy was knocking them out with his product, selling bundles and bundles of these things called butterfly ladders. People seemed frantic as they waved their twenty-dollar bills at him. Moving closer, I watched mesmerized, itemizing each part, knowing I had to have them in my booth.

At the end of the day, I went to the booth, introduced myself, and soon discovered I knew the promoter, so I told the pitchman to tell his boss I wanted to meet and discuss wholesale possibilities. Shortly afterwards, my phone rang, and John was on the line. Being an ex-pitchman himself, he started pitching how much his booth grossed and how well the product was selling on the West Coast, where I lived. Although his wholesale price seemed very high, I told him I'd like to place an order for an upcoming show in Hawaii and that I needed samples immediately. To my surprise he suggested that I could buy some from his booth. This suggestion ticked me off because usually if a person is about to spend a few thousand, he's given samples. Not John.

I bought twenty and headed back to California with the flimsy pieces of unique plastic design. Three feet long, a foot wide, and a quarter-inch thick, the funny-looking piece had me excited. Its figure-eight rings ran down the middle of a frame, making two rows of raindrop-shaped holes. Pulling fabric through the holes in whatever shape might be desired created window treatments that needed only to be attached to the wall with a few screws. Several could be used for a large window or one could be cut for a small one. These ladders made elegant do-it-yourself window dressings for any house, saving thousands over having curtains or drapes made professionally.

In California I met a manufacturer friend who'd already knocked off the infamous thigh master, calling it the thigh buster, so he knew what to do. Scandalous as copying may be, it's done every day. Holding no allegiance to anyone, I soon had Brian's eyes and head spinning as I pitched him on the money we could make. We pooled our finances and started a company and changed the raindrop shapes into circles to avoid patent infringement. Then we brought in a lawyer at 10 percent of our company, saving us the ten thousand dollars retaining fee he originally asked for, and that is how our Create.A.Curtain business was launched.

As I pitched the lawyer, telling him how rich he would be when this product took off, I remember sitting in my office with speakerphone blaring and chopping out a line of crystal meth. *How weird,* I thought. *I'm standing on a gold mine with one foot in the grave. I'm talking to a lawyer and my partner on a conference call speakerphone about the riches we can't imagine, yet living the secret life of a strung-out junkie.* The facade seemed invincible, but darkness neared. I had spun out of control twice in the previous ten years and twice landed in rehab, making amends and pretending to be rehabilitated. After all, I was a faker, a pitchman who could sell ice to Eskimos. Convincing friends I had recovered was peanuts—I just learned to hide using drugs better, using them in private and never overloading.

Brian and I bought our first injection mold costing fifteen thousand dollars and soon had it running, but even before we had a single curtain maker ready to ship, we had presold thousands. Word travels fast in this business. The butterfly-ladder company put a commercial on TV, and we rode its back like a tick, always keeping our prices a shade lower. With the pitch season lasting from May to the end of Halloween, we decided to buy four more molds, three of which we sent to Tijuana, Mexico. TJ, as it's commonly called, could produce the stock for much less, and since it was only a couple of hours from my home, I took the responsibility of keeping an eye on the Mexico plant. Weekly trips to TJ, always by limo and always with drink and drugs down and back, made me feel as if I were really somebody, and I began to flash cash and live wildly. Money flowed in, and I had only to sit at home with a phone and fax machine pitching to promoters to buy my curtain maker. This was big-time pitching, but the concept didn't change. The customers couldn't live without the product, I had only a few left, and they needed to buy quickly before the product was sold out.

Amazing how things change but still stay the same. Our molds ran around the clock, and the money flowed in. Three molds in Mexico and two in Los Angeles put out thousands of pieces a day, each at a cost of less than twenty cents, which we sold wholesale for two dollars. The pitchmen sold them at three for twenty dollars, making everyone a winner.

My dream had come true. But still, in the quiet of the night when phones stopped ringing and the fax machine stopped chirping, I went to the bathroom to get high. I remember sitting on the stairs that overlooked the living room and fireplace and expensive furniture and stereo equipment wondering what in the world I was doing. I was so torn by my double life that I hated myself. So to silence that small voice, I'd roll another joint or take some pills. Meth to wake up, pot and pills to go to sleep—day after day. My addictions had enslaved me.

Chapter 10

ARRESTED

In the summer of 1993, Create.A.Curtain panels were selling like hotcakes, practically falling off the shelves, and the stores couldn't keep them in stock. A manufacturer has no better feeling than to have his phone ring off the hook with the frantic cries of sales people begging for more merchandise. The chirping of the fax machine spitting out order after order wakened me, soon the phone chimed in, and I'd be up and off, forgetting breakfast, reaching for a soda, and doing a shot of speed, which left me spinning all day.

I really thought I was the man—legitimate business during the day and drug dealing at night with money coming in every day, all day. I tried to keep the two separate because I didn't want my partner or legitimate business associates to know about my nightlife. Not having to leave my house and doing business by phone or fax while lounging in my backyard seemed beautiful. Often I'd pinch myself to make sure it was all real. I'd be weighing out a couple of pounds of pot while talking on the phone to a distraught store manager desperate for Create.A.Curtain panels or doing speed while discussing profit margins by phone with my partner, living two lives with the candle burning at both ends.

As days turned to weeks, so did my days turn to nights. More drugs and dealing and less legit business made me struggle harder to rise in the morning, and I'd let the answering machine pick up the calls. Logic and reason began to fade as I usually survived on only a few hours of drug-induced sleep, and my caution also waned. I'd call my partner at noon, after listening to several frantic messages, only to lie about being out of town taking care of business. My mind no longer cut precise lines through business decisions, and often I'd be speechless on important matters. Methamphetamine is a wickedly addicting drug, and California is one of the biggest producers. I didn't realize that my home, Temecula, was right in the heart of meth country.

At night I'd stop in bars to drop off pot and play pool while soliciting new customers. Before long these customers began asking if I sold speed also. Of course, my greedy mind began running through the numbers, weighing the potential profit with the risk of selling, a risk much higher because of the clientele. Pot smokers are usually lazy, sleepy, docile, and easy to sell to. Speed addicts are the opposite—often jittery, unpredictable, and violent. They are always scheming and plotting to get their next fix. They have no boundaries because, as their need increases, their morals and lifestyles deteriorate.

I decided to buy some speed and give selling it a try. I'd been using it for a couple of years, so I knew where to buy it and get started. Within the first week, I knew speed was the bigger, quicker moneymaker, so before long I switched from selling pot to selling speed. The speed world is unique because users seem to go underground during the day. Shielding themselves from the sunlight with tightly drawn curtains, they wait for dusk to fall. I used to be amazed when I drove through a small village called Quail Valley. During the day streets were empty, but as night fell, the place came alive. By midnight a visitor could see pale, skinny folk mowing their lawns, fixing cars, and riding bikes, often with flashlights taped to hats and handlebars.

Outsiders didn't always know this night subculture even existed. Paranoid and skittish, these "tweakers" resembled living corpses as they walked aimlessly through the night looking for any possible way to secure the next fix. Then, like a knight to the rescue, I'd come driving through in my convertible BMW or shiny red Corvette holding exactly what they wanted. Some, recognizing my car and knowing whom I sold to, would come on foot and bike, hoping for a fix. I dealt only in quantity, so most of the tweakers had to buy from the ones I sold to, as I rarely dealt directly to any of the strung-out addicts.

My inflated ego made me laugh and shake my head as they tried to talk me into a sprinkle of euphoria by offering stolen merchandise, sex, and even food stamps just for a fix. I'd brush them off like a king would a peasant and in my arrogance bask in their pitifulness. (God forgive me.)

One night on my way home after dealing drugs, Rich, one of my customers who actually had become somewhat of a friend, phoned me on my cell. Slobbering drunk at a bar, he told me he needed a ride. Knowing Rich and how he'd usually start fighting and end in jail, I weighed the cost of bailing him out and the cost of his being unable to sell for me for a few days and decided to turn around. He waited outside with a beer in each hand, and I cringed, knowing any one of the parked cars in the dimly lit lot could be cops waiting and watching. He hopped in, and I slowly drove onto the street. Checking my mirror intently as I drove, I didn't notice anything unusual behind me, but about a mile from my house at a crosswalk, I caught a glimpse of a parked patrol car. Rich, oblivious to everything, promptly took a drink of his beer right in the lights of the crosswalk as we drove by. Instantly I saw the lights come on as the patrol car edged out of its hiding place.

"Rich, you idiot! We just passed a cop," I yelled. He instinctively rolled down his window and, without thinking, threw out the two open beers. Now I was crazy with anger! The cop had several reasons to pull us over, but the least of my worries were a drunken friend and a couple of beers. Almost immediately the flashing lights appeared, my throat tightened, and I began to panic. *Should I step on it, turn at the next corner, and try to throw out this bag of speed?* I wondered. I made the decision out of indecision, stuffed the bag between the seats, and pulled over as the lights flashed in my rearview mirror. Trembling, I rolled down my window when the officer approached with his flashlight.

"Good evening!" He said abrasively, probing the beam of his flashlight to and fro in my car. "You two been drinking?"

"No, sir," I stammered, "I haven't had nothing all night. Just taking my buddy home from a party."

"Get out of the car," he ordered. "Go stand in front of my patrol car and don't move."

Oh God, oh God, I began. *Please don't let him search that car. Oh God, oh God, please,* I prayed fervently as if God and I were everyday pals and it was His job to once again save me from my corrupt lifestyle.

Holding his flashlight the cop searched through my car, and soon he returned with something in his hand. I could hear my heart beat as if suddenly amplified into my eardrum. Weak-kneed, I watched in horror as the policeman opened the bag.

"What have we here?" he asked sarcastically looking directly into my eyes, which were blinded by his flashlight.

"I've no idea what you have," I lied. This response only made him angrier.

"Oh, so you don't know that this is methamphetamine and possession is a felony?" he hissed back.

"I've no idea what you are talking about," I said again, and then a thought popped into my mind. Without hesitating I said, "The car belongs to my girlfriend, so I've no idea what's in it." Still praying as I lied, I knew that this whole thing could become even worse if I were not careful because just under the floor mat behind the driver's seat lay a black automatic handgun, fully loaded and unregistered. Drugs are one thing, but drugs and guns together are exponentially worse.

Then the officer pulled out handcuffs, and for the first time in my life I felt the chill of steel wrapped around my wrists. He sat me in the back of his car with my friend Rich, and when the tow truck arrived for my car, we sped off into the night.

I could not believe I'd been arrested. Images of jail with riots, rapings, and stabbings filled my mind. I'd never been to jail. Having just movies and hearsay to go on, I immediately concocted the worst scenarios imaginable. Arriving at the Riverside County Jail, I was charged, printed, photographed, and stripped. The experience seemed surreal with muffled voices, the clang of steel doors slamming, the filth, and the smell of old sack lunches. A couple of hours later, an officer led me to a holding cell plastered with graffiti. Several phones hung on the wall, and immediately I grabbed the closest one. Putting the filthy receiver to my ear, I began frantically dialing home. After several rings, the beautiful sleepy voice of my savior whispered, "Hello?"

I didn't waste time. "Misty, I'm in jail, busted for possession of speed." Silence on the other end. I instantly got upset and began barking orders. "This is no time to start getting mad! I need your help now!"

The sleepy voice began speaking calmly and rationally saying, "Calm down. I'll get you out as soon as possible." We talked a bit more and then said Goodbye. With the voice on the other end gone, I once again felt the awful, suffocating feeling of total helplessness. This wasn't me. I couldn't be sitting in a filthy cell in a two-bit jail.

About 4:00 A.M. a guard moved me to a tank where inmates are housed, and I heard doors slamming open and shut. He gave me a toothbrush and bar of soap, along with an entirely too big bright-yellow jumpsuit and shower shoes. Then he led me through the tank to a cell door. I heard a buzzing sound. Instantly the door popped open, the cop pushed me in, and just as quickly the door slammed shut behind me. As I looked around in the dim light, I couldn't believe my eyes. In the eight-by-ten, two-man cell with two bunks against the wall, unless my eyes deceived me, I wasn't the first or second or even the third man in—I was the fourth in this tiny cement box. I stood by the door wondering what to do, not wanting to be any more of a nuisance than I had already been by waking the sleepers. Slowly sliding down against the closed door, I sat right in front of the disgusting toilet. With no possibility of sleep, I listened to the sounds of the night, wondering how this disaster could have happened to me.

At 7:00 A.M. the doors opened with breakfast. I shoveled what looked like dog food into my mouth as the men informed me it was called SOS, or "Slop on a Shingle." With breakfast over, I went to the phone. Misty had been up since I first called; she was on top of the situation, and I silently marveled at her strength and loyalty and lack of condemnation for my stupidity. Hours later a voice on the loudspeaker announced, "Fleck, roll it up—you're going home." My yell of relief sounded as if I'd just done twenty years. Soon the gate opened, and I was only too happy to leave. But when the cops returned my clothes, a strange thing happened.

As soon as I got into my clothes, I also got back into my old way of thinking. The fear and stench and shame of jail disappeared like mist, and my mind forgot the joy of being released and focused on the world of drugs. Before even leaving the jail, with my sickness never far from the surface, I began planning where to go and calculating how much speed I'd need to replace what had been confiscated. Again I put my head up and shrugged off the humiliation of being busted as I walked out of the jail with my faithful girlfriend, Misty, who was fighting back tears.

They can't touch me, I pumped myself up. *I'm smarter and quicker,* I silently mused. My buddy Bob waited for us outside, and with a smile and a hug, we hopped into his vehicle and drove home. My car sat in the driveway, and as we pulled up I asked if everything was still in it. Misty's glance begged me to shut up, and she said simply, "I put the 'thing' in your closet."

"Good girl," I said as I patted her on the head as if she were a pet. "I need to take care of something, and I'll be back in a bit." Jumping in the car without consideration or thought of what she also might have been through, I drove down the street, callous, conceited, self-centered, inconsiderate, and cold, quickly becoming someone no one would want to know.

I drove to the connection's house, picked up another bag of speed, and did a couple of lines just to get back into my normal state of mind, completely failing to wonder how the officer could have missed the gun in my car. I'd bought the gun from some guy I didn't even know, and one could only imagine where it had been or what it had done. Even in my madness, Jesus still answered my prayers, still giving me chance after chance to acknowledge Him and turn from evil.

About that time I began having a strange recurring dream at night where I'd be standing in a field looking toward the horizon. Although the day would be sunny, the horizon would be inky black, and darkness would begin to slowly roll in like a thick fog. The sun would dim and soon be engulfed by this blackness. I'd wake up terrified and shaking. Unable to fall back asleep, I'd lie there trying to shake off this evil, almost tangible nightmare. Little did I know that soon my daylight would be thrust into darkness, and evil that I couldn't have imagined knowing would become a reality.

Chapter 11

INTO
THE NIGHT

After the arrest I found a lawyer listed in the yellow pages who specialized in drug cases. I set up a meeting, paid him a few thousand, and, convinced by his confidence that he could get me off with minimal discipline, I continued to deal speed. Quantities doubled and tripled until I was selling several pounds a week. Paying five thousand dollars a pound and turning that into eight to ten thousand for each pound, stacks of money were changing hands daily.

Misty now knew about the drugs, but I assured her I wasn't using, just selling. She cried and pleaded with me to quit, so I'd give her a two-inch thick stack of bills, telling her to go buy something nice and quit worrying. Many times I sent her on the road to work a fair just so I wouldn't have to listen to her. When she was away for weeks at a time, I really became transformed into the likeness of those I was feeding. I adopted a couple tweakers who, for just a few fixes a day, would do anything I asked. One cleaned my house, washed clothes, and made beds while the other ran errands, fixed cars, and delivered drugs as needed. They answered my phone as if I were running a store and took messages so I could sleep. Often I'd be too loaded to talk to anyone intelligently, so I'd give him or her the "take a message" sign. My days were getting shorter and nighttime became my domain.

The lawyer showed up one day to discuss my case when I was loaded, sitting in the backyard with my "servants." Ordering them to fix my lawyer a drink, I escorted him to my office. With a peculiar look on his face, he asked me what I did for a living. I pointed to a pack of Create.A.Curtain and said, "Those are mine." He looked in disbelief and said, "What do you mean?"

"I own this product," I said. "Have you seen them on TV?" He nodded. "Well, I get a piece of every one that sells, and we're selling tons," I boasted, totally full of myself.

"Really?" he nodded trying to believe me.

Reaching over my desk to grab a cigarette, something fell out of my pocket. To my embarrassment, there lay a personal baggie of speed, right at the lawyer's feet. I looked at him, then to the baggie. Darting around the desk to pick it up, I sheepishly stuffed it in a drawer. His previous look that I had assumed was admiration instantly changed to pity. He stared at me, and although never saying anything out loud, he shook his head. My appearance must have made him sick. He saw a gaunt, shirtless junkie who, through some stroke of luck, could have had a perfect life but was desperately trying to sabotage it.

The lawyer laid out my defense and with it the possibilities, both pro and con. I listened, but nothing really sank in. I wasn't worried; I lived in a fog and continued to believe that I wouldn't have any serious problem. How could I? I was the man. People paged me and called me 24/7. I was needed. I couldn't fail.

We went to court, and just as the lawyer predicted, the judge gave me a suspended sentence, providing I complete a drug program called Drug Diversion. I would have to meet three times a week for six months and be subjected to random drug testing.

As soon as I heard that, I knew what to do. Normal people would be thanking God, straightening up their lives, and sobering up. But I contacted a friend who I knew didn't use drugs but needed money. I told him I needed a favor and would pay a couple thousand for him to show up three times a week and sit for an hour in a class educating drug addicts. He said, "Sure," so that was taken care of. The next class didn't begin until December, four months away.

My drug use was going up day by day, and soon I talked to my business partner only a few times a week because all our customers now ordered Create.A.Curtains directly from the plant. All orders were online, and we simply deposited checks and watched, making it even easier to stay out all night and supply drugs to dealers. By this time I had sales for quantities larger than my first source had available, so I had to find a bigger connection.

Through an acquaintance I met a quiet, well-connected man from south of the border. Mario, who always dressed in clean, creased, and pressed clothing, became my new supplier. On time and polite, speaking very broken English, he always had lots of product. He'd come to my house a couple times a week with a duffle bag in one hand and two or three young enforcers always flanking him. He'd smile and shake hands. Because he didn't smoke pot, rarely drank, and almost never did speed, he did not appear nervous or jittery, as do most speed users.

When we met, I tried to act sober, not wanting to appear the junkie I was. I started to admire this drug dealer, but each time he came, a little more illegality would follow. At first just pot and speed, but soon came cocaine and heroin. I wasn't interested in them, but I noticed how he felt more and more comfortable with me and stayed longer at my house. One night he showed up with two extra-large cases. After we finished our business, he asked me for a favor. What could I say? I was dealing with a member of the Mexican Mafia who basically had adopted me and trusted me as a business associate.

I said, "No problem. What do you need?"

He opened both suitcases, and what I saw made my eyes bulge. Neatly packed inside lay the biggest assortment of firepower I had ever seen: revolvers, semi-automatic handguns and, to my amazement, even machine guns, the likes of which I'd seen only in the movies. He saw my shock, laughed, and asked, "See anything you'd like?" Stammering, I began picking them up, caressing them. I didn't bother asking where they came from, just how much they cost. He rattled off various prices. But he wasn't trying to sell to me. He pulled me to the side and quietly asked, "Rick, there's a guy who wants to do some business. Is it OK if he comes over so we can take care of it?"

Inside, my mind said, *No! No! No! This is too much.* But the line had been crossed, and now weapons were involved. Who knew whether those guns had been used in killings and whether a simple sale of guns could erupt into a deadly robbery? All these thoughts flashed through my mind. Mario must have seen the apprehension, so he said, "It would really be a favor to me, and I don't forget favors." This I had heard was very true about Mario. He didn't forget favors. I was now stuck. Crumbling inside, I hesitantly nodded approval, and he smiled, patted me on the back, and said, *"Bueno, bueno."* The four sat in my living room to wait.

Later that evening, a knock on the door startled me. Mario's smile faded—his hand disappeared behind his back and under his shirt to retrieve a chrome-plated automatic handgun. Almost on cue his three enforcers produced menacing looking weapons, terrifying me. But trying not to show fear, I walked to the front door. *What am I doing?* I wondered silently. *Oh God, oh God. Please don't let anything happen,* I repeated over and over.

Peering through my peephole, half expecting a blast to tear a gaping hole through me and the door, I could see a large, fit, military-looking Caucasian with a flattop haircut. Motioning Mario to the door, I stepped aside as he looked out. Upon seeing the face, he signaled to his men to put away their weapons and, tucking his into its hiding place, his face transforming into a smiling, gracious host as he opened the door, welcoming the man. Rambling on about nothing, he cordially tried to make everyone relax. Still shaking, I wanted this night to end. The evening's events had crossed a line even in my drug-induced fairy tale facade of invincibility, and I felt afraid, very afraid.

Their business completed, Mario prepared to leave, shaking my hand repeatedly saying, *"Gracias, gracias."* While I knew I had made a mistake with these dangerous men, I wouldn't know how bad a mistake until some months later.

After a few days my friend Rich showed up wanting some speed to sell, and during our superficial banter he smiled and said, "So you're in now, huh?"

I didn't know what he meant, so I asked, "What do you mean?"

He said again, "You're in. You're one of them now."

With my smile fading and seriousness taking over, I demanded to know what he meant—exactly! He backed up and with no smile said in an all-business tone, "You're in with Mario and the cartel."

"Hold it right there," I snapped. "What makes you say that?"

"I've heard it on the street," he replied.

Once he left, I sat down and tried to make sense of things. *How can it have gone from selling a little pot to make some extra money to this? Is it as bad as Rich said, or is he mistaken? Does Mario think of me that way? Oh, I hope not,* I thought.

One night Mario showed up unannounced, looking paranoid, his eyes darting back and forth. Looking disheveled, with mud on his expensive boots and his shirt untucked, he pulled out his gun and set it on my table. Without saying a word, he then went into the bathroom and began washing his hands and face. His enforcers were also silent and nervous. When I asked what was going on, Mario shrugged and replied, *"Nada, nada,"* but looking into his eyes, I saw evil. The look startled me because I had not noticed the evil before. He looked at me without a word, just stared.

Taking a second look at his shirt, I saw that it was covered with tiny red splatters. Seeing them, I looked once again into his eyes and said, "You better get another shirt."

He went into the bedroom and soon reappeared wearing one of mine. "I'll get you another one, Friend, don't worry." He labored a smile. Just as suddenly as they'd appeared, the four disappeared into the night. Again alone, I tried to make sense of the recent events in my life. Obviously Mario and his men had just done something unspeakable. Although they didn't tell me what, several weeks later I heard of a shoot-out a few miles away. Chills ran up my spine when I recalled that night.

Now in the eye of a hurricane, it seemed I couldn't escape. Fearful, I began carrying a gun everywhere and soon had several stashed all over my house—under my bed, under my couch, in the closet, in the garage. Paranoia took over, and I had a security system installed, complete with motion-detector floodlights both front and back. A small minicamera imbedded in the wall provided a picture of anyone standing at my door, and I'd sit in my office watching the monitor for hours, staring motionless, imagining sounds in the night. When neighborhood cats activated the lights in my backyard, I'd jump with fright, grab the nearest weapon, and crawl to the window and wait for the enemy to appear. They never did.

Chapter 12

ALONE

Friends came around less and less frequently. Misty spent much time either at her mom's house or on the road working. What must have gone through her mind as she watched me deteriorate into a night crawler, a paranoid evil shell of a man she once loved and respected, a man who had deteriorated into someone unrecognizable?

One morning in late October when I returned from my nightly drug deliveries and deviltry, Misty was awake and surprisingly friendly. It seemed odd because lately she'd been distant, always worried, and often confrontational about my lifestyle. She'd pleaded with me several times, expressing her fear of Mario and his men when they showed up and invaded our home. I'd tell her we were much safer with them as our friends than as enemies. She begged me to move someplace else. We had the money and could have bought a place wherever we wished, but I just couldn't leave the scene behind. The black fog in my dream crept closer and closer, but I seemed powerless to escape.

That morning she tucked me in bed with a light kiss on the cheek and said, "I love you." Then she left the room, closing the door behind her. About three in the afternoon I awoke. Drowsy and needing a fix of speed to wake up, I got out of bed, opened the door, and yelled out to Misty. No answer. Wiping the sleep from my eyes, I stepped into the hallway and looked down into a vacant room—a room that the night before had been filled with pictures, pottery, plants, a sofa and love seat, and a stereo. Now the room was bare, cold, and empty. I staggered to the top stair and sat down, wondering whether I was dreaming. I began to yell, "Misty! Misty! Misty! Where are you? Misty, help me; please help me." No response broke the silence that followed.

Eyes blurred with tears, I noticed that on each stair leading down to our living room lay a page from my alcoholics anonymous book. On the bottom step lay a small stack of books I'd read many years before when I first met Misty while recovering from a drug-rehab program. And now, only these books were left, pleading for me to turn from my ways. On the top of the small pile of books, Misty had left a handwritten note. I read it, already knowing what it said. She'd finally given up and decided to save herself from a fate she could see fast approaching me.

I sat there in tears, numb and alone, blaming everyone and everything else but myself, and even yet I could not see clearly enough to get help. I called a friend, told him I needed a few things, and ordered him to come over. Misty had taken my guns, probably in fear of retribution, so the first things I bought were guns. Then I called Mario, telling him we needed to meet. I don't know why, but at that moment, instead of turning my life around, I became even more hardened. At this point, I believe God made a next-to-last-ditch effort to open my eyes. A sober person who has found God's patience beyond comprehension, but I spat in God's face.

The next day an old friend of mine from Canada, whom I had known since grade school, phoned. Colleen's voice sounded so far away and foreign. Misty and I had spent a lot of time working with her at fairs throughout the years. She'd call occasionally to check up on us and let us know of new products and supplies, but she had no clue about the recent happenings in my life. Sensing something wrong, she pried and coaxed, so finally I spilled my guts. But instead of the complete truth, I told her Misty had left and taken everything for no reason. I heard Colleen gasp as I rolled out obscenities, describing how I'd been taken to the cleaners. She tried to calm me, but the more I talked, the worse I sounded. Soon she hung up.

From that point on, my remaining self-restraint vanished. In a small village nearby, all-night parties with plenty of women were common—sex is bought, sold, and given away. AIDS is common, and not just from IV usage. Uninhibited sex with multiple partners is the norm in the meth and coke world.

A woman named Penny came over one night with some stolen stereo equipment trying to trade for drugs. I already had boxes of stolen stuff that tweakers had brought over, hoping to exchange for a fix. But she shocked me by bringing her ten-month-old son with her. Feeling some unexpected compassion, I sold to her. I always wondered why I even bothered with her boxes of junk and a few hundred dollars cash in exchange for an ounce or two. I normally did not sell ounces—too small for my ego and just as much risk as selling pounds. But when Penny showed up, I'd let her in. One night she pulled a little black bag from her purse. Curious, I asked, "What's inside?"

She hesitated and said, "You don't want to know."

Of course that piqued my interest, and I demanded to know. Just as Satan tempted Eve, he now tempted me and, without caring, I fell headfirst into his deadly trap. She opened the bag, revealing a black onyx ring about three inches in diameter, some feathers, beads, and a candle.

Puzzled, I asked again, "What are they?"

Then she dimmed the lights, pulled up a chair, and told me about her mother and other family members who practiced black magic and witchcraft on the back streets of New Orleans. This story instantly attracted my attention. Because I had been raised in a Christian home and had attended Christian schools, I never had experienced any sort of occult practices. My eagerness and willingness must have shocked her. I wanted to see Satan and what he had to offer. She warned me again, but I said, "Count me in."

She took a strand of my hair, laid it on a little stand that held the candle and onyx ring, and began mumbling while looking at me and into the air. Closing her eyes and swaying from side to side, she mesmerized me with her ritual. When finished, she put her trinkets away and gave me a chilling warning. Seeming to look straight through me, she said, "Every guy I've known has ended in jail. Be careful."

Feeling nothing, I laughed and pretended not to take her warning seriously. But I soon would remember those haunting words said in the candlelight.

A few days later while lying in bed, I heard what I can only describe as the sound of a breeze rustling through tree branches. Soon fully awake, I tried to tune my ear to identify it. The air-conditioning? An open window? As I began looking around, it would come and go, sounding louder but then fading off into silence. It came back a couple of days later, and this time I recognized it. Off and on for the next few days it came and went. Then one night Penny showed up unexpectedly with her box of charms, trying to exchange it along with some cash for drugs. After we completed our deal and did some speed together, I told her about the noise. She immediately said, "This is your spiritual guide who has come to live with you."

I said, "You're a liar," and laughed, but she didn't laugh. She was serious.

A few days later when I was once again alone, this breezy sound came through the house. I immediately said out loud, "Who are you?" Unexpectedly, from out of thin air, came a tiny, barely audible voice. At the same time a cold chill came over my body, and what felt like icy pin pricks ran up my spine. I said again, "Who are you?" but this time I whispered in fright.

I heard a female voice, very distant and hard to understand; at first I was too petrified and stunned to understand her words. But I began to ask questions and soon learned that she was the spirit of a long-dead prostitute who had lived in the 1800s. She told me her name and the city where she once lived, that she was here for me, and that all I had to do was call her. Off and on throughout the next few days, I'd feel the same cold, prickly sensation and know she was present. I'd call out, and she'd answer. I'd quiz her and test her, asking all kinds of questions, and she'd respond to some but stay silent on others.

The next time I saw Penny, I couldn't contain myself. "Penny, you are not going to believe what happened!" I exclaimed.

Before I had a chance to tell her, she said, "You've met your guide." But her next words floored me; she told me the spirit's name, her previous occupation, and the city where she once lived, clairvoyantly perfect in every detail.

Up until that point, each time I spoke with the demon posing as my guide, I would wonder if I actually were losing my mind. Was this real, were the daily doses of meth finally making me crazy; could I possibly be hallucinating? Penny's words confirmed that I did have my own spiritual guide. Knowing I now had an eye in the sky led me even deeper toward destruction. The darkness of my heart matched the moonless nights. With evil music playing, I'd drive the neighborhoods dressed in black, carrying a gun at all times. The paranoia changed to insane boldness and calloused cunning, making me feel truly invincible. (God help me.)

Chapter 13

TOTAL
DARKNESS

One day Mario's right-hand man, Clavo, phoned saying Mario had been in a high-speed chase with the car I had rented for him. The cops had caught him and seized more than fifty thousand dollars in cash and probably two times that amount in drugs and guns. *Oh no!* I thought. *What am I going to do for a supply now?* But Clavo said he wanted to do business with me, and I immediately saw dollar signs. If I secured another connection, I could supply Clavo, who by default had inherited Mario's customers. These customers would mean a new surge of money, not to mention ego. So I told Clavo Yes, and within an hour he arrived. I made some calls and found another connection in Long Beach, an hour away, so I began doing business with him. Clavo took Mario's customers but bought from me. Since it was my connection, I'd go to Long Beach to get a supply, and we'd meet on my way back to settle up.

Some time later, Clavo and I were pulling out of the parking lot of my bank. Always on the lookout for cops, Clavo spotted one moving slowly along in the adjacent parking lot. He tensed. "Check it out, Rick," he said, motioning slightly with his head toward the patrol car. I glanced quickly and calmly eased out into traffic. I looked in my rearview mirror as I pulled onto the main street, and sure enough, the highway patrol followed, staying several cars back. As soon as I turned onto the ramp that merged into the interstate, flashing red lights filled my rearview mirror. I swore and said, "Clavo, we're being pulled over." He looked at me with a deadly stare and said, "I won't be taken in." Not fully understanding what he meant until he flashed me a glimpse of the black steel tucked into his pants, I thought, *Oh, Lord, this can't be happening.* I pulled to the side of the road and stopped. The highway patrol eased in behind me, and a moment later a large police officer emerged. I knew the routine and had my fake smile and driver's license ready.

"Hello, Officer, what seems to be the trouble?" I asked while handing him my license. Standing with his hands at his waist looking at me through mirrored sunglasses and chewing on a half-smoked cigar, he let out a sarcastic snort.

"You are. You're the trouble, Punk!"

Not bothering to take my license, the policeman leaned over, placed both hands on the door of my convertible, and said, "Fleck—you think you're really special, don't you?"

I sputtered, trying to disagree, but through a barrage of obscenities, he advised me to shut up. I sat there speechless as this highway patrol officer I had never seen before called me everything but a human and spared no use of his four-letter-word vocabulary. During his tirade he informed me "they" knew who I was, where I lived, and what I was doing. "They" also were just waiting for the right time to take me down, and no amount of Mexican protection would save me. This he directed at Clavo in no uncertain terms.

Still holding my license, I sat stunned, saying nothing as the officer turned on his heel, walked to his car, and disappeared into traffic. I looked at Clavo, who once again relaxed, and I said, "What's up with that?"

He shook his head and said, "They're on to you; it's time for you to move."

Was this one last attempt by my guardian angel to warn me? Was Clavo's warning really true or just an attempt to intimidate me? I thought about it the rest of the day but once again dismissed the advice, deciding I was untouchable. The cop's warning fell to the wayside. I told people of the cop's words and laughed, vowing never to be caught.

Strangely enough, after that encounter, when I delivered drugs or drove around my pick-up area, I'd often see the same car or cars and the same faces appear on street corners and at traffic lights. I'd wrack my brain trying to remember where I'd seen them before and then blow it off as just paranoia. *This isn't the movies,* I'd rationalize. *No way can "they" be tailing me. I'm too smart to get caught.* Often I drove in circles and exited at off-ramps just to see if I could catch anyone tailing me. Although several times I could have sworn someone was following me, I never did catch anyone. However, "they" weren't strung out on speed, and "they" obviously had a plan.

By this time I talked to ghosts, saw ghosts in the rearview mirror, and looked like a ghost who would have scared anyone who had known me in the past. I wore only black clothes and black boots and moved only in the dark of the night. Because I neglected to pay bills, the electricity and the phone and heat were off, so one night I strung an electric cord to my neighbors' house and plugged it in, unknown to them. My life had spun so far out of control that I now lived in an unfurnished house with a couple lamps and a few candles, which spread an eerie glow through the night. Using only a cell phone and pager, I had deteriorated into nothing but a drug dealer. I had lost touch with my Create.A.Curtain business partner after weeks of his leaving messages on my pager, desperately trying to reach me.

Increasing the frequency of my trips to Long Beach, where I picked up my supply, I began spending time meeting drug dealers and users. Orange County is a beautiful area. I remembered having attended the drug rehab in Long Beach during the eighties, and, ironically, I now spent much time driving on the same street, looking at the same ocean, and smelling the same sea breeze that once gave me so much pleasure in my sobriety.

Finally, admitting that the cops were probably on to me in Temecula, I began looking for an apartment to rent in Orange County. I figured I'd move and blend into a different scene, hoping to lose the fear of always being followed. I found a place in a quiet area about ten minutes from the beach, a two-bedroom apartment in a complex with a security gate and underground parking. It was a far cry from my lavish two-thousand-square-foot house on a golf course, a place that held such terrible memories that I'd often crumple in tears thinking about it; then I'd immediately do a shot of dope to escape.

I paid the deposits, moved in, and immediately called for my spirit guide; on cue she whispered in my ear. She was my companion, and we talked incessantly. The second day I set up a drug deal and, against my better judgment, allowed the buyer to come over. I had sworn to myself that nobody would know my new address—I'd be safer that way as many people by this time knew me, and my name was also on the books of the drug task force in Riverside. I hoped to stay incognito and just do deliveries, bringing nothing and no one to my home. But my greed and ego prevailed, and I invited a trusted dealer to my home.

Dean showed up that evening, and after a little chitchat left with a bag of meth. Thinking nothing of it, I went out and did my rounds from Long Beach to Riverside, which often took a day or more, making all the stops like a black-clad Santa delivering poison. I returned home in the early morning and called Penny, who had not yet been to my new apartment. She came with donuts and coffee and surprised me when she said, "Happy Birthday." December 7 is a day I'll never forget for many reasons.

"Birthday? Is it really the seventh?" I asked astonished. Time for me had become a blur. No longer were there colorful weekends, happy appointments, or anything that made me genuinely smile. Drugs and money—that was it. Days blended into weeks. I sat for a few minutes trying to remember what a birthday used to mean. Family, friends, presents, cake, love . . . I checked my voicemail. "Hi, it's your mother. Hi, Rick. We love you. Happy Birthday! Please call, please," the message ended. A tear crept down my cheek, and with it a flood of memories from innocent days gone by.

"Rick, Rick." Penny's voice snapped me back to reality. "There's someone at the door."

I finally heard the knock. For a drug dealer, an unexpected knock at 7:00 A.M. when nobody knows where they live, usually means the worst. Picking up my gun and setting it just under the edge of the couch, I motioned for Penny to see who had come to the door. My mind began to run down all the possibilities— none good. The apartment had a security door at the front, and no one could enter unless a tenant buzzed them in. Whoever stood at my door had gotten past the security. *Cops? Robbers? Landlords?* I waited nervously as Penny peered through the peephole. "It's Dean," she said, looking at me.

I motioned for her to let him in but was immediately shocked at what I saw next. Dean entered my apartment, moving quickly but cautiously around Penny. Following him were two men I'd never seen. Scanning the living room, Dean approached me nervously, saying nothing. At about three feet away, he suddenly pulled a gun from under his shirt and stuck it in my face. Shocked, I stood motionless, wondering if this were really happening. Was it a birthday joke? Instantly the other two men stood over me. I could feel cold steel against my temple, and looking out of the corner of my eye, I could see all six chambers of the revolver packed with death, possibly my death.

Dean instructed me not to move. He sent Penny to the bedroom and shut the door. Then he grabbed my cell phone and told the others to look for drugs. Now the scene started to make sense. They were robbing me! This was a home invasion, strong-armed robbery, and I was the victim.

I had heard of dope fiends robbing their connections—not a bad idea in the drug world. What drug dealer is going to call the cops and report the robbery of his drugs? I should have known I'd be a prime target. Too flashy, too cocky, and too strung out on my own supply had made me careless and an easy prey.

They rummaged through all my clothes and soon found a large wad of cash. Further searching turned up my gun, which had been within my reach the whole time. They kept threatening me, demanding to know where to find drugs. My fear turned to anger as they continued to search my belongings.

"You're really screwing up, Dean!" I yelled. "That money isn't mine—it belongs to Clavo!" I was hoping they'd realize it wasn't me they were actually stealing from.

Dean paused, his sleep-deprived eyes glazed, and said, "Tell Clavo he's burnt!"

"Don't do this. Don't do this," I said over and over.

After a few more minutes, Dean stopped tearing through my things. He walked up to me and put his sweaty face inches from mine. I could smell the alcohol on his breath. "Look, Stupid, you're out of your league. Give me your dope and then go back to where you came from, or I'm going to hurt you."

Then I looked at him and made a cold statement, "Kill me. Kill me. I'm already dead anyway."

That seemed to stop the searching. Dean's accomplices pulled him away and said, "It's time to go."

"Let's tie him up and take him someplace. We'll dump him where nobody will find him," Dean begged, but the two others said, "No! Let's get out of here now!"

They disappeared just as quickly as they had entered. I cursed and cursed as reality set in. Still in shock, I tried to formulate a plan, but in my stupor, I couldn't think straight. I felt rage, but rage mixed with terror. What should I do? I told Penny to leave as I paced back and forth in my living room. My options were all grim, but the one option that I didn't even consider would have saved my life as well as the lives of others. I should have gone far away—home to Alberta. It wasn't too late. To simply have left would have been the best choice, but I wasn't the Rick Fleck who had come to California in search of the good life. Now I was only a cheap imitation and empty shell of a once-energetic and promising young man. The demon-possessed, drug-addicted junkie's mind had been given over to darkness.

I left my apartment and phoned Clavo, telling him what had happened and what Dean had said. Clavo told me to get a hotel room and wait for him. I did and waited and waited all day, battling fear and rage, but oblivious to the chain of events that had been set in motion. Sitting on the bed, I reached over and pulled open the nightstand. As always, a Gideon Bible lay in the drawer. I blinked and hesitantly reached for it. It felt strange in my hands, and with it came memories of days long gone. As I glanced over the pages, I repeatedly caught sight of words and phrases that indicated some type of change. "Leave what is behind. Let go of falsehood. Repent before it's too late . . ." These phrases kept flashing through my mind. It seemed that words on that very page I'd turned to warned me to change. "The time is fast approaching. Change, change." Stunned, I convulsed with sobs until I fell asleep.

The sound of pounding eventually roused me. Taking a moment to get my bearings and blinking off the sleepiness, I stumbled to the door and peered out the peephole. Clavo and two hooded figures stood outside my door. Still shaking off the cobwebs of sleep, I opened the door, and in came Clavo and two men I'd briefly seen in the past. Sitting down, they wanted to know exactly what had happened. Realizing the seriousness of the situation, I began trying to downplay the morning's events. None were interested in any softening; they wanted to know where Dean and the money had gone. I had no idea but knew he'd stayed at his sister's in the past, and Clavo said, "We could check her place." Then I asked a couple of questions that will forever haunt me. "Clavo, what are you going to do if you find him?" He shrugged and looked at the other two. Again I asked. Finally, with no answer from them, I said, "It isn't worth anyone's life. You aren't going to kill him, are you?"

The question hung in the air a moment until Clavo said, "Of course not. We just want to get the money back and rough him up a little. That's it."

Believing they were telling the truth, I left with them, and we soon arrived at the trailer park where I'd previously visited Dean's sister. At just past midnight I pulled up beside the unlit trailer— odd for a place that sells drugs. Clavo and the others looked uneasily at each other and slowly exited the car. One said to me, "You make sure you're here when we come out, or you'll be sorry." Terrified, I sat in the car. A light mist fell, forming little diamonds on the windshield.

The thunder of gunfire suddenly ripped apart the quiet night. Bright flashes of light blazed in the darkness. I froze in the driver's seat. Then I heard a guttural voice whispering, "No, no, no. Please, no, no, no." The sound continued to crescendo until I could hear myself screaming hysterically, "No! No! No!" as I pounded on the steering wheel.

Any rational person would have driven straight to the police, if a rational person would have been in such a situation in the first place. But I didn't move. Suddenly silence, and three hooded figures came flying out of the trailer, hopped into the car, and yelled, "Get out of here! Go! Go! Go!" Still in shock, I sped off into the night.

Once onto the street, I heard myself still screaming "No! No! No!" Crying hysterically, I yelled, "What did you do? What did you do?"

No one replied. Driving aimlessly, I finally calmed enough to ask what had happened. Clavo said that someone inside drew a gun, and they all opened fire. No one knew how many had been shot, but obviously in a shoot-out like that, only horrible things could have happened. They told me to take them to a hotel where they could shower and lay low until morning. I was more than happy to drop them off, and as they were getting out of the car, Clavo said, "Don't contact me for a few weeks or until this blows over." He stared at me fiercely and icily added, "Oh, yeah, don't say nothing to nobody about tonight." He shut the door and left me alone with the horror.

Chapter 14

RUNNING WITH
THE DEVIL

The next few days went by like a blur. I got in touch with my connection in Long Beach hoping to make a buy, but he'd heard of the shoot-out and said I should find someone else to deal with. Later, I picked up a newspaper and learned the extent of the bloodshed that awful night. The words *double homicide* jumped out at me. "Oh, God, please don't let this be what I think it is," I whispered to myself. As I read, the terrible reality finally set in. Two people had tragically lost their lives, and I was in big trouble.

I gasped as I read the newspaper article over and over. Not sure what to do or where to go, I drove around for hours. I hadn't been back to my apartment, fearing any one of many scenarios that included police and revenge. At that point I was running out of options, so I turned to my two constant companions, drugs and my satanic-appointed guide. I checked into a rundown budget hotel in Lake Elsinore, a few miles from my old home in Temecula. Contacting an old connection, I bought some speed and filled a few orders for people who'd been paging me. Penny paged me and showed up a few hours later. She told me about developments in Orange County: Everybody knew I was involved, and the police were rounding up suspects. Penny shook her head saying, "I told you so; every guy I've told about the black magic has met terrible circumstances."

I sold drugs from the hotel for a few days. Then late one night, after getting high, I heard a noise next door. I intentionally had rented a corner room, as drug dealers often do, so only one side of the room has to be watched. I had a stethoscope so I could listen to sounds in the next room occasionally, checking for cops or anything out of the ordinary. I listened intently for a few minutes and heard nothing. Thinking it strange but admitting that I might be paranoid, I temporarily dismissed the fear. Several hours later I saw a figure walk by my window. Instantly on pins and needles, I crept across the floor to peer through the drawn curtains. The sidewalk was empty.

I became increasingly agitated and suspicious so decided to fix the problem. I called the front desk and strung the desk clerk a long story about expecting family from out of town and said I needed to secure the adjoining room. He stammered and hesitated oddly, replying that I couldn't rent it but giving no reason why. I again demanded to rent it. Again he said No. Slamming down the phone, I stormed to the lobby. Ranting, I quizzed him up and down as to why I couldn't rent the room. He sat there looking scared and pale but not giving in. Getting nowhere, I stormed back to my room just in time to catch my pager. The number on the screen sent a cold chill down my spine—Clavo. Not wanting to believe it, I stared blankly at the number. *What should I do?* I asked myself. I did nothing.

Soon daylight broke. I hadn't slept for several days, surviving on speed, and paranoia pushing me to the breaking point. Again the shrill ring of my pager startled me—Clavo's brother's house. Quickly I called, and to my surprise heard Mario's familiar broken English. He told me about his arrest and few months in jail and that his lawyer had pulled strings to get him out. But what he said next took my breath. He slowly asked if I'd seen Clavo lately. His tone told me he knew something. I paused, thinking about how to respond, knowing Clavo had just paged me the night before. Might Clavo be there with Mario now?

After a few seconds of trying to gather my wits, I told Mario I hadn't seen nor heard from Clavo in several days.

Then, still guarded and probing, Mario asked another strange question. "Are you and Clavo OK with each other; are there any problems between you?" This question sent off all kinds of bells. My paranoid mind spun, and a thought I didn't like crept into my head. Might it be possible that Clavo planned to silence me? After all, I was definitely the weakest link, had much to lose, and didn't commit the crime—so I could potentially rat them out to save my own skin if I were arrested. I really began to lose it at that point because I knew firsthand how deadly this could turn out. I assured Mario that Clavo and I were fine and that I'd come see him soon.

That night my pager went off again, and again that same number stared at me—Clavo. I went to the phone and called. Hearing it ring on the other end made me nervous. What was I going to say? He had to know I would be shaken and scared. Would he want to see me? I knew I didn't want to see him.

"Hello—this is Scott."

Not fooled by the alias, I recognized his voice and replied, "Hey, it's Rick. What's up?"

"Hi there, Buddy. How have you been?" His voice sounded jovial.

"OK, I guess." *How can he sound normal after what has happened?* I wondered silently.

"So what's happening?"

I shuddered at the sound of his voice and tried to muster a response. "Nothing much," I stammered through a dry throat.

"Where are you staying?" he probed.

"Oh, just wherever—you know, no place in particular," I dodged the question.

He rambled on for a moment about nothing and then came another question. "I need some speed. Do you have any?"

"Yes, I have a little, but I'm waiting for some more right now."

Instantly he was interested. "I'll take what you've got now—*where are you?*"

A second red flag waved. He wants to know where I am, I shuddered silently. *He's never before been this persistent. . . . He doesn't do business at night. . . .*

"I need that stuff, Rick. When can we meet?" the voice on the other end persisted.

"I've some things to do right now. How about later tonight?" I stalled, hoping he'd chill out. Then the third flag was unfurled.

"OK, Rick. Check it out. I want you to meet me at 'the ranch.' Do you know where it is?"

The ranch—panic tightened my chest. I'd heard this "ranch" mentioned in hushed conversations. I knew it as a place in the hills where people disappeared. "Um, no, Clavo. I don't know what you are talking about," I lied.

"Well, look. As soon as you're done with your business, call me. I'll give you directions. Hey—it's important. OK, Buddy?"

His voice smiled, but every nerve in my body screamed, "Stay away!" I had a terrible feeling inside that I might soon die. "OK, Clavo, I'll call you soon," I lied again, hanging up.

Then I went out to my car and drove aimlessly into the night, back and forth on roads I'd traveled during the past two years. I went to the beautiful lake where Misty and I had enjoyed watching the moon dance across the ripples. I drove by our house and remembered all the promise and dreams we once had but that now lay shattered and dead. I drove and cried and yelled at the voices in my head, sinking deeper and deeper into desolation. I found myself gripping my automatic handgun, flipping the safety switch on and off, and pointing it at myself in the mirror.

I returned to the hotel at about 3:00 A.M. and lay on the unmade bed clutching my gun. With my free hand I opened the nightstand drawer and found another Gideon Bible. Cursing at it, I opened it and said the most foul and evil things as I scoffingly read through some texts. I remembered hearing when growing up that the unpardonable sin was blaspheming the Holy Spirit, so I did my best to curse and blaspheme and say in no uncertain terms how much I hated God. Yelling and crying out loud, waving the gun and putting it to my head, I had reached the lowest point a man can be. Angrily I ripped the Bible in two, opened the door, and hurled it into the street. Slamming the door, I walked back to the bed calling for Satan to reveal himself. Then I made a statement I'll never forget. I screamed, "Satan, I know you're real. God, if You're real and truly want me, I'm up for grabs. You decide and show me who's more powerful."

With that I chambered a bullet in my gun, put the barrel in my mouth, and tried to pull the trigger. My finger wouldn't move as I tasted steel on my teeth and felt the gun barrel in my mouth. I pulled it out, waited a moment, and tried again. Either I was too cowardly to end my life, or Jesus Christ had just taken control from Satan. I lay there shaking, tears streaming down my face, and then I heard a strange, muffled noise. Next came a knock, and I quickly asked who was there. A voice said, "Danny," but it didn't sound familiar and I didn't know a Danny who'd be coming over. Walking to the door, I peered through the peephole, seeing nothing. A split second later, the door came crashing down and chaos broke loose. Pitched backward, I went airborne for a moment until the door and several masked, armed men fell on top of me.

Terrified and disoriented, I heard voices yelling; but not until I had the barrel of a gun pressed hard against the back of my head and several knees crushing against my spine did I realize what had just happened. Busted again! Oddly enough, I had a strange sense of relief. Cold metal quickly encased my wrists followed by the clicks of handcuffs closing. Taking off their masks, the cops congratulated themselves with jubilant shouts and high-fives for bagging a trophy. I felt like a mouse in a trap. Every officer involved in the bust crowded into the little room, exulting that they'd protected society from an evil creature.

I watched them, unable to say a word but wishing I could just go home, hug my mom, and leave this nightmare behind. The cops ransacked the room searching for money, drugs, weapons—anything a criminal might have. Another cheer went up when one found a bag of drugs and a couple of guns. I secretly breathed a sigh of relief my captors were the police and not Clavo or any of his crew.

The next few hours were devoted to questioning me as I sat cross-legged on the floor with cuffs digging into my wrists. Representatives from several agencies were present, and each took turns interrogating me. At first I thought the arrest was about the previous week's horrible events, but as I listened, I soon realized this was a drug bust, not a murder investigation. Drug Enforcement Administration (DEA), Alcohol, Tobacco, and Firearms (ATF), Immigration and Naturalization Services (INS), and others involved in a drug task force peppered me repeatedly with questions about drug associates, but no one mentioned murder. Although obviously I was in major trouble, my ego and pride would not give up. As I looked around, my head swelled thinking of how much attention I was getting. *All these people are here because of me. I'm a celebrity now.* What sick psychotic thinking could make a person believe he was cool in that situation? Perhaps it was one of Satan's delusions to mask the fact that I had reached bottom and had nothing to live for.

Soon the interrogation ended, and I once again found myself in a cold, dirty jail cell waiting to be processed. This time there would be no Misty, no bail, and no way out.

Chapter 15

LOST BUT NOT
FORGOTTEN

Fleck, Fleck," a sharp voice pierced the cold silence. I blinked into consciousness. Stupefied, I tried to piece the last twenty-four hours together.

"What in the * * * " Four-letter expletives exploded from my mouth.

"Oh no!" I mumbled to myself remembering my little walk to the toilet a couple of hours earlier. *So it wasn't a dream. I really am lying on a cold cement slab in a filthy cell.* A cold blanket hit me in the face before my hands could react. Next a lunch skidded to a halt on the floor in front of me.

Any meth user knows that getting a good night's sleep rarely happens. Most of the time users just come to in an idling car, a strange house, or a park bench. Sleepless days and nights meld into weeks, and when the body can take no more, the mind simply shuts off. For an hour or a day or longer, the user lies motionless. Then suddenly, without warning, the corpse blinks, and slowly the cycle begins again.

"Eat up. We'll be back in a while to get you," said a voice followed by the slam of a door, leaving me once again all alone.

I devoured everything except the bag, leaving what seemed an even sharper pang of hunger in my stomach. The blanket, tossed in with the lunch, appeared to be about the best and definitely the smelliest friend I could have wanted at that point. Instantly I lapsed into dreamland again only to be awakened abruptly by a deputy, who handed me a bedroll including a jumpsuit and towel, and a "fish kit," a small bag containing soap, toothpaste, and toothbrush.

He motioned for me to follow and without a word began walking down the hall. After an elevator ride and several turns down a hall, a door creaked open, and the sound of my new home hit me with a blast—blaring TV, voices, and the nonstop slapping of dominoes hitting steel tables blended together in a jailhouse cacophony—or symphony, depending on how long a person's been inside.

The din quieted as all eyes followed me to my cell. Trying to look unafraid, I shuffled into the cell, and the door clanged shut behind me. Two steel bunks hung to my left. A small desk welded to the back wall undoubtedly had witnessed the tears and prayers of many who, like me, would have given a limb to be anywhere else. The once-white walls, now nicotine-stained to tan, enveloped me. The sink and toilet in the corner reminded me of how far I'd fallen. *I've owned bathrooms bigger than this cell,* I thought silently. The type of fear that engulfed me was new. Completely out of my element, I felt totally helpless. While my body detoxed, the next days passed as a blur of sleeping and eating.

During that time I called my business partner from Create. A.Curtain, who sounded relieved that I wasn't dead. "Brian," I began, "I'm busted, in the county jail, and in big trouble. I need a lawyer, and I don't want money to be a hindrance. Find the best and send him ASAP." Brian didn't delay, and within a day I had my first attorney visit.

"Fleck, you got a visit," boomed over the loudspeaker, and when my door popped open, I shot out of bed, not stopping to brush my teeth or splash water on my face. I stumbled into my jumpsuit and shuffled to the door of our tank. When the door opened, the officer motioned me down a hall and into a room containing several booths with phones. Choosing one, I sat and waited, not knowing whom to expect. When the elevator door opened on the other side of the glass, a tall, extremely well-dressed man appeared carrying a leather briefcase. Seeing no one else, he strode toward me and sat down, eyeing me cautiously. "Mr. Fleck?" he questioned.

"Yes," I said.

Still looking unconvinced, he began, "Your partner, Brian, contacted me on your behalf and said you are in trouble. My name is Mike, and I am here at his request."

I could see already that this man would be expensive, and *that* I liked. Still living in a fantasy, my head swelled as I bragged about my position as owner of a large company. Not thinking of how silly I must have appeared with my uncombed hair, ashen face, sunken eyes, and bright-orange jumpsuit, I continued building my facade.

"How much?" I finally asked.

Without batting an eye he replied, "Thirty thousand dollars, and that . . ."

I stopped him in midsentence. "Whoa, whoa, whoa. I thought you said *thirty thousand?*"

His eyes narrowed, but he kept his composure. "Fleck, that is my fee," he restated matter-of-factly. I saw a flash of moxie. He wasn't the least bit intimidated. I liked what I saw and said, "OK, half now and half when it's over. Brian will be sending you a check."

He paused calculatingly, and then shrugged, "OK, we'll do it that way."

We talked some more, and then he left as he had come, still looking as if he'd just stepped out of the glossy pages of *GQ*. I felt confident and soon learned that he was the best—but the best might not be good enough for the trouble I was in.

Christmas approached quickly, sped up by my days of recuperating sleep. While in the dayroom, I overheard a couple of guys talking about a Christmas program a local Christian church put on every year in the county jail. I sneered at the thought of those hypocrites peddling their lies of happiness. Hatred simmered as I thought of all the churches, schools, and prayer meetings I'd attended throughout my early years. Being raised in a Christian home, I'd played the game, faked a relationship, but now I served Satan and knew he was real. As the men kept talking, the mention of a box of chocolates and Christmas candy caught my attention. I listened intently—food. I'd do anything for food, never mind candy. Wasting no time, I found out the scoop and decided to go.

On Christmas Eve we were ushered into the chilly little chapel smelling of musty books, and I quickly went to the back but not before first making sure the gift boxes were visible. I hated these people, but I couldn't place the origin of my anger. I listened to the story of Baby Jesus, the manger, and the wise men without feeling a thing except discomfort. Their words meant nothing to me. Cold and hungry, I wanted it to end. The Christmas carols felt like sharp barbs, and I ached to break free.

Soon the program ended, and the boxes were passed out. I could not get out of the chapel fast enough. Back in my cell, I immediately dug through the box, touching and smelling the colorful candies, oranges, and chocolates. My celly and I laughed and made fun as we gorged ourselves. Soon only a little brown pocket New Testament and a pamphlet from Set Free Prison Ministries remained with the crumbs. I looked at the Bible and wished it were an Almond Joy® or Snickers®. A voice told me to throw the Bible away, but I didn't. I closed the box and slid it under the bunk.

Christmas Day came and went with tears and paralyzing depressions. I glanced at the TV in the dayroom only to see a commercial advertising Create.A.Curtain. The sight made me want to kill myself for being so foolish.

The day after Christmas I felt overwhelmed with the urge to look in my box. I pulled it from under my bunk, opened it, and sat staring in silence at the little Bible. Flushing with anger, I mentally growled, *What am I doing? I've read this trash before. It's boring and a bunch of nonsense.* Finally I picked up the little book and thumbed through the pages that smelled faintly of chocolate. Then I set the empty box on the floor and lay down, Bible in hand, opening to the first verse of the first chapter of the rest of my life.

I don't know when I stopped reading, but for the first time in years I had a peaceful night's sleep. No rustling, no cold icy murmurings from my spiritual guide, although that would change. The next morning, as soon as I finished breakfast, I began reading; and when I got to Matthew 4:18, 19, where Jesus called the disciples, I felt a tugging, a longing to belong to something that mattered. Tears welled up in my eyes, and soon I found myself on my knees with my face buried in my bedroll and hands tightly clasped together. "Oh God, oh God, help me please," I began. "Please forgive me, forgive me," I repeated over and over again with my body convulsing in agony. I gave myself to Jesus, my beloved Creator and Redeemer, the One whom I'd spat on and despised for so many years. He then reached His nail-scarred hands down into the deepest, darkest pit of demon-infested hell and gently pulled this lost sheep to safety. With ten thousand times ten thousand angels rejoicing, the Savior once again raised the dead, giving me a heart of flesh.

Tears still roll today as I write about this act of extreme grace, something I did not deserve and never will fully understand but with a trembling soul accepted. December 27, 1993, became the first day of a life truly worth living. Thank You, my Lord.

I have since heard that after conversion, a new believer rides on a pink cloud, and this explains my elated almost carefree attitude in those early days of nursing spiritual milk. I began reading the Scriptures daily, and little by little the Holy Spirit brought to mind some of the teachings of my childhood in an Adventist home. I enrolled in the Set Free Prison Ministry course from a mainstream Protestant group. Immediately I ran into a myriad of questions. I was born again and learning new doctrines but becoming more and more confused. I knew for sure that I loved Jesus and wanted to know the truth, but my confusion, stemming from childhood experiences, continued to grow.

One experience will illustrate: One day when I wore a necklace to school, the teacher said, "You can't wear your necklace here."

"What do you mean, 'I can't wear a necklace'?" I spat at my teacher in defiance.

She replied with jaw set, "Take-it-off!"

I walked away burning with anger, thinking of all the nasty mishaps I hoped would befall her. How dare she tell me I couldn't wear a necklace and threaten punishment if I did?

I hated the school, the teachers, even the religion! I was tired of the rules, regulations, and threats of expulsion and hell. The more I pondered my Christian education, the more senseless it appeared. *Maybe I should just obey their rules to make them happy,* I decided. *If I appear to be a good kid, then all will be well. Or I can be myself, do what I wish, and face their wrath and scorn. Either way, I'm not going to heaven.* I told myself that I just wasn't good enough. Even if I played the part and fooled everyone around me, I knew I couldn't fool God.

I imagined a God with folded arms and a scowl looking down at me, the One commanding His sin-counting angels to be sure every wrong is logged. Finally I decided to throw my fears to the wind and ride the wave of self as far as it would take me. Why not? I wasn't going to heaven anyway, so why miss out on all the fun?

Where did this concept of an ogre of a God come from? I remembered the pure feeling I had when coming up from the cold water of baptism at age ten. I felt so warm and happy. All my family watched, some with tears in their eyes, as my face shone with happiness. Who stole that sunlight? How did that kind, merciful God disappear?

An enemy, Satan, knows that if he can alter the motivation for obedience, he wins. He caught me in the same quicksand that he used to trap hundreds of other kids in the seventies—legalism. We were taught the law before the relationship, but without love for Jesus and the power of the Holy Spirit, obedience remains impossible. Honest children and young adults were trapped in failure and despair. Few of my peers knew that salvation is by grace through faith!

I wasn't taught the good news in school. I didn't recognize it from the pulpit. How was I to know? And therein lies the key—we are to know by searching the Scriptures ourselves. By the time I decided to turn my back on God, I could read, study, and make sound choices. In high school I excelled in class but failed to read the plain English of the Bible. Why? Ah—that's where Satan's covert plan begins. "Those who are deceived by Satan look upon God as hard and exacting. They regard Him as watching to denounce and condemn, as unwilling to receive the sinner so long as there is a legal excuse for not helping him" (Ellen G. White, *Christ's Object Lessons,* p. 204). Without reading for myself, I became convinced that religion is a lie. Centuries ago Satan tried to keep God's Word hidden, and today he plays the same game in a different stadium. He allows enough religion to keep people pious but not enough truth to save their lives. Looking back, I blamed parents, teachers, preachers, and others—but sadly, it was my fault. I didn't search the Scriptures for myself. I tried many of the world's vices but ignored sound advice for myself.

Ten years of running amok landed me in this place tailor-made for thinking—jail. With plenty of time and many long-suppressed emotions to revisit, I set out to prove once and for all that the Seventh-day Adventist Church was a deluded cult. I mounted a white horse, grasped a blazing sword, and decided to rescue all the misguided Adventists and free their poor souls from captivity. I planned to mop the floor with their vegetarian health ideals and expose the myth that Ellen White was a prophet.

Now in a cell, I studied all the mainstream Bible studies and resources I could find. All these Sunday keepers couldn't be wrong, I assured myself. I wrote to several Bible instructors repeatedly asking for explanations on Sunday as the day of worship, the state of the dead, an eternally burning hell, and other doctrines. Time and again they'd write back with vague answers, supported only by tradition and fragments of Scripture.

I began to get nervous; my research wasn't revealing what I'd hoped. By now I'd given my life to God, considered myself a born-again Christian, and begged my fellow Sunday keepers to give me the ammo required to silence the Seventh-day Adventists' arguments. But it didn't happen. In panic I prayed, *Can it be possible that those people, the ones who shook their fingers at me, are right? Oh, God, no, don't let it be!*

After searching the Sunday keeper's doctrines, still fully on their side, I thought it only fair to look at the Seventh-day Adventists' beliefs, too, and began with *Steps to Christ*. I'd prove that Ellen White was a legalist and send a ripple throughout the Adventist Church. Through the night and into the morning I read, unable to put the little book down. How could I have overlooked the gentle, loving truth found throughout the book? If Ellen White was the Adventist light bearer and these words were true, then I sincerely had been deceived with my understanding of Adventist beliefs. Adventists believe the Bible and all the goodness and grace it holds. Sure, a few misled individuals had influenced my life and I, looking for an excuse to rebel, used their ignorance in my defense. Sadly, I didn't bother to study for myself.

After finishing *Steps to Christ*, I rethought my life. Puzzle pieces seemed to fall into place. The doctrines I'd tried so hard to prove wrong held up, the hatred I'd felt so strongly now dissipated, and I praised God for His mercy and patience with my toxic attitude toward Adventists. I learned to let the dos and don'ts fall where they belong—behind a relationship with God, not as a means of salvation. With the cart squarely behind the horse, the good news was even better than I imagined.

I realized that all the commandments hinge on love, love for God, who isn't a sin-counter with a checklist. Heaven is not a place reserved for the good. If it were only for the good, then Jesus' death counts for nothing. He shed His blood for our sins. This is Good News! My debt is paid; my mansion is waiting!

Chapter 16

BABY STEPS TO
GIANT FEARS

I wish I could say that everything was perfect and worry-free after I gave my life to Jesus that day. I actually thought that, in some magical way, all my problems would suddenly disappear. I'd beat all the charges and walk out into sunshine. Those thoughts would prove to be illusion—strictly fantasy.

Although I had a new heart cleansed by the blood of my precious Savior and I knew that if I died I would awake to see His glorious face, I also still had every ounce of rage and hate and evil challenging my infant belief. The Bible speaks of a battle raging between good and evil, flesh and spirit, and the unseen forces warring for human souls. I had been snatched from the fowler's trap, but Satan wasn't going to give me up without a fight.

The demonic spirit, clothed as an innocent spirit guide, made its presence known. Voices, whisperings, and icy cold episodes within my cell and mind were his attempt to scare me back. Gone was the soft, appealing voice of the woman who had been my companion; instead, the true character of the evil imp became clear. Upon realizing this, I began praying that Jesus would please take this parasite from me. Again and again I prayed when the rustling sounds of evil began, asking to be freed from the oppression. I would imagine my tall guardian angels at the door to my cell holding swords of fire to ward off the evil intruders. God delivered me from the spirit I had allowed to oppress me. Praise God! As I write this book, I cannot remember her name; I've tried, but I believe the Lord has wiped the name from my mind and will not allow Satan to reestablish even the knowledge of the name. Glory to Jesus!

I believe this act of deliverance, which was the first of countless more, set the foundation in my newly converted mind of the mighty power of God. Many satanic events had occurred prior to my arrest, proving to me the power of Satan and his agents. I will not recount them but say only that any force with the power to stop Satan's delusions and manifestations is the power I want to have watching my back and guiding my feet! Knowing Satan, then watching God crush his control over me, convinced me of a Power far greater. How much more will it be on that great day when Lucifer and everything he has done cease to exist? But I only had begun walking on the narrow path that leads to heaven and would yet encounter many, many devastating, yet faith-building roadblocks. My fears of the past continued to plague me; the seeds I'd sown still germinated, and they soon would grow to produce heartbreaking fruit.

Reading the Bible daily and being filled with the Holy Spirit gave me a new adventure. I'd wake up, look at the cement walls, and try to find a reason to live. Before long the little brown Bible would be in my hands, and a reason would appear.

The morning after I gave my life to Jesus, I called Mom and Dad to give them the good news, and when I told them of my conversion, all I could hear were sobs and more sobs. After hanging up the phone, I went back to my cell and cried like a baby. Finally, I had made them happy, and it felt good. My lifestyle choices had been a devastating blow to them. They had worried and prayed for me for many years. To a bystander my situation may have looked bleak and hopeless, but to my parents, Jesus had given the ultimate answer to prayer.

One day a guard called my name over the loudspeaker in the dayroom. "Fleck, get ready for an attorney visit." Always excited to see my attorney, I hustled to prepare—brushing my teeth, washing my face, combing my hair, and heading out the open gate. But something seemed different this time. Instead of the doors to the visitors' rooms on the left, a door to the right opened, and the control guard told me to take the elevator to the ground floor. Questioningly, I looked at him, but received a blank stare. I walked a few steps to the elevator, stepped in, and the door closed quickly behind me. Instantly I felt queasy as the elevator sank to the floor. There a guard escorted me to a tiny cubicle. Sitting on the stool, I stared through the inch-thick glass into the vacant cubicle waiting for the lawyer. Suddenly the door behind me swung open, and without warning two unfamiliar men entered my tiny space and shut the door. Terrified, and having no room to move, I stood up and pressed back into the glass partition behind me. They grabbed my shoulders and pushed me back down onto the seat. Still holding me down, they came even closer. Just inches separated our faces. I could smell their breath and cologne, and it felt as if a hundred-degree wind had just blown through, making me sweat profusely.

One of them produced a mini tape recorder, pushed play, and set it behind me on the little ledge. Without introductions, the other leaned right into my face and asked, "Where were you the night of December seven?" My heart pounded. *This is it,* I thought silently. *They know, and I'm finished. Oh, God, help me.*

I stayed silent, but my eyes must have given me away. They pressed on with question after question for what seemed ages but was really only seconds. I remained silent. This only caused them to crowd me more. I thought they were going to hit me, but they didn't. Finally, after a couple of minutes, I burst out almost in tears saying, "I want to speak with my lawyer!" The statement seemed to stun them a bit because, as if slapped, they both moved back silently. Seeing the reaction, I said again, louder, "I want to speak with my lawyer!"

At this point one of them picked up the recorder, pushed stop, and tucked it back into his pocket. The other pulled out two cards and set them on the narrow ledge. Never losing eye contact with me, he said in a low, menacing voice, "Fleck, we know you did it, and we'll prove it." His voice grew louder but never lost its lethal tone. "We'll be waiting for you; it may not be today or tomorrow or even next month, but we'll get you and take you down. I guarantee it." Nodding at his partner, he opened the door, and they disappeared as quickly as they'd come.

Shaking and sweating, I sat there terrified, finding it hard to breathe. I wanted out badly but could only sit and think. *How can this be? I didn't do it. They have to realize I didn't do it—no, not me. I'm a farm boy from Canada, not a cold-blooded killer. It's not me; it's not me.* At this point I knew I'd need a miracle. Dealing drugs was one thing, but murder was entirely another. I picked up the two business cards and read, "Orange County Homicide" and their names and numbers.

Then the door opened, and I returned to my housing unit. Seeing me visibly shaken, my celly asked what happened. "Nothing," I said, and lay down, staring into space wondering, *What am I going to do now?*

After breakfast the next day, I sat at the desk in my cell and wrote the whole account of exactly what happened the night of December 7. A couple of days later when my lawyer visited, I slid him the account of that terrible night. Not knowing what it was, he brushed it off and said, "I'll get to it later."

"No," I insisted, "read it now and silently." Surprised by my abruptness, he began to read. His eyes widened, and he lowered the pages, looking around as if he might be watched, and continued reading.

When finished, he lowered his voice and asked, "Who have you told this to?"

"Just you," I replied. Then I recounted how the two detectives from Orange County had tried to squeeze me a few days earlier.

Before tucking the pages into his suit pocket, he said in a hushed tone, "You've hired me for a drug case, not this," he pointed to his pocket. "This is bad, real bad. But I'll do some checking for you," and he shut his briefcase, smiling a strained and uncomfortable smile. His words didn't help; neither did his demeanor.

Back in my cell, I begged God to help me, reciting all the texts I could find about His answering prayers if we ask. Although prayer had been foreign to me, surprisingly, I felt comfort from knowing what a powerful God I served. Every day brought more worry, but worry prompted me to pray and read the Bible. From prayer and reading grew faith and serenity, even if for only a short time. I'd never before felt such peace.

But as soon as I lost my focus, the devil ferociously attacked, condemning and killing my newfound joy. Days were filled with hills and valleys aplenty, a roller coaster of emotions.

Dealing with sobriety had never been so hard. I ached to use. I'd relive getting high and dream of being loaded, but when I'd wake to the sounds of jail, all reality came rushing in. But the silver lining made me smile because for one more day I was saved and sober. I can't remember how many times I'd toss and turn while dreaming, reliving the scandals of drug use and then praying, "Oh no. Oh please let this be a dream. Please don't let me use meth again." Then, waking to the sounds of prison, I'd thank God to be inside. I soon came to the conclusion that I'd rather be locked up and sober than free and high.

After about a month, I had my first real court appearance. The judge read the charges: "Possession of methamphetamines, possession of cocaine, possession of firearms, possession for transportation, possession for sales, violating probation, failing to appear for drug program . . ." His voice droned on in the stuffy courtroom. After hearing the offenses, I pled "Not guilty" as instructed by my lawyer, who had told me that everyone pleads not guilty. While the proceedings continued, I scanned the unfamiliar faces in the courtroom until I saw two familiar faces that startled me. I could feel sweat creeping into my palms. There they were, the two detectives from Orange County, sitting quietly at the back, staring intently at their prey—me.

Later, my lawyer laid out the whole deal. The felonies I'd been charged with totaled a possible seven years. I just about fell over when he dropped that bomb on me, but that was nothing compared to his next statement. He'd been in contact with the Orange County officials, who had yet to file any murder charges. The two cases were separate, and the homicide detectives were there only to make sure I didn't try to bail out. If I did raise enough to bail out, they would file murder charges, which would prevent any possibility of bail. "They aren't going to let you go," my lawyer said glumly. "If they file those charges, you could face the death penalty."

I blinked a few times and asked him to repeat the last part—the death penalty. His voice trailed off again. *This can't be happening.* I sat numb and silent searching my lawyer's face for a sign of hope but found nothing.

"Be patient. Sometimes these things have a way of disappearing over time," he said without conviction. I clung to those words. *Be patient. Be patient,* I kept reassuring myself as I returned to my cell.

I don't know how many times I prayed, asking God to fix this mess I'd created, but to these prayers I heard only silence. Psalm 23 became one of my favorites, and I'd hang on every word: "Fear no evil . . . fear no evil." Satan fought to discourage me, but the words I read each day overpowered his attacks.

During this time I began to write. I'd probably not written a letter with any substance in my whole life, but now, with much spare time, I found writing therapeutic. So, I began making amends to everyone who came to mind. I prayed God would let me recall those I'd sinned against. The list became agonizingly long, but letters had to be written. Surprisingly, letters of shock and encouragement trickled in as those to whom I'd written responded, making my heart sing. Forgiveness, what a wonderful act!

To my amazement, many other people I hadn't heard from in years wrote, sending encouragement and scriptures for me to read. I felt love from many places that I had shunned and avoided in the past. My so-called friends from the drug world disappeared, but, amazingly, the true servants of God sent letters and prayers. I saw a side to Christianity I only had heard about in the past. Letters talked of prayer circles all over the country with little groups petitioning God on my behalf. *With these people praying, God is going to deliver me,* I assured myself. These friends strengthened and reassured me that God's will would be done. But a lesson I had to learn over and over was that my will and God's will often were miles apart.

Chapter 17

GROWING
PAINS

Soon I settled into the day-to-day routine of county jail.

Dawn broke with sounds of doors opening and the smell of food permeating the air as porters (inmate workers) began unloading steaming breakfast trays from large carts. "Chow time! Chow time!" blared over the loudspeaker, and clanging doors opened revealing sleepy-eyed, grumpy men who would rather still be in dreamland, the only true escape.

With more men than tables, we new inmates (called "fish") had to sit on the floor and choke down repulsive-looking food. Pecking order in county jail usually is determined by the amount of time served. Some had been fighting their cases for months, even years, giving them the most "juice."

We were given ten minutes to eat, usually enough time because the portions were small and most of us were starved from lack of food during our drug-induced daze on the streets. Then "Go home! Take it back to your cells!" would boom over the loudspeaker, signaling the meal's end. A few nods and "See ya's" would suffice for the early morning pleasantries before we returned to the cells and under the covers for a post-breakfast siesta. By about ten most men were up and buzzing on too much coffee. The doors would clang open, releasing us for the morning dayroom time. In the dayroom were several four-seat tables and two benches located in front of a blaring TV. Everyone had his own little program—some lined up for the phones while others waited to shower.

Two tiers with ten cells each made up our tank. Every hour the cell doors opened, giving us a chance to go in or out as we chose. The door openings were called "in lines." Some inmates liked cell time without their cellies. Usually I would shower and then go to my cell, spending quality time with God and my Bible. While trying to ignore the dayroom racket, I'd muse to myself, *I don't belong here.* My reclusive manner and unwillingness to assimilate kept me in the dark about jail customs.

Oblivious at first to prison mores and used to being in control, my mouth occasionally put my well-being in danger. One day as I returned from a lawyer's visit, a skinhead named Shawn, who liked to play jokes, aimed his playful attack at me. As soon as I entered the buzzing dayroom where card games, dominoes, and TV entertained the men, a loud voice addressed me, "So, who were you ratting on today, Fleck?"

Not sure I understood him and hoping he'd not repeat it, I pretended not to hear. But now, with everyone's attention focused on my reaction, Shawn yelled again, "Hey, Fleck, who were you telling on today?"

This time I heard it clearly, and my blood started to boil. Shawn had no idea what kind of nerve he'd struck. Just returning from an attorney visit and having discussed the murder charge, my emotions, not my mind, were in control. In addition, Shawn's insinuations, if in fact true, could cost me my life. Without much thought and little hesitation, I unleashed a fury of expletives, capping them with a demeaning racial slur.

Instantly the din in the dayroom ceased, leaving only the sound of the TV and thick tension. *What now?* I wondered. As I watched, Shawn moved down the tier toward me, clenching his fists. He meant business. Looking toward the observation booth and the guards, I noticed one pick up the microphone and announce, "Dayroom recall. Dayroom recall. Dayroom recall." The buzz of my cell door popping open never sounded so good. Shawn slowed and, pointing at me, cursed loudly, telling me that when the doors opened, I would pay.

Terrified and shaking, I quickly shut the cell door. My celly sat on the bed looking at me. Shaking his head in disbelief, he said, "You messed up, Rick. You really messed up," over and over again, not helping my peace of mind.

"What did I do?" I asked almost in tears.

"You could have said just about anything to Shawn because he was only kidding. But when you used a racial name, you crossed the line. Shawn's a skinhead, and skinheads hate anything not a skinhead. For you to call him what you did, he's left with no choice but to hurt you bad."

My celly's words drilled into me as I sat wide-eyed, finally understanding why everyone in the dayroom froze upon my tirade. Crawling on my bunk, helpless and terrified, I quickly began talking to the one constant Companion who'd always listen. "Oh, Lord, please forgive me . . ." I began with hands clasped tightly. My new relationship with Jesus and His promises to protect me were my only hope. *Will God bail me out yet again?* I agonized silently.

Before long, doors popped open, and the guards blasted, "Dayroom time. Dayroom time," over the speakers. With my heart in my throat, I stood at my door waiting. Shawn's door popped open, he looked at me, and spewing words describing my demise, he came to my door and said, "Get inside." I reentered with Shawn behind me.

Is this really happening? Am I going to die? God, please help me, I silently screamed.

Slamming the door, Shawn pulled out a shank, a razorblade melted into a toothbrush, and crouched low with hands out to his sides. He began taunting me and moving forward. Backing up slowly, I started apologizing. "Shawn, I apologize. I'm sorry for what I said; I didn't know you were joking." Apologies continued out of my mouth as the space between us closed. "Shawn, I won't fight you. I'm a Christian," came as a last-ditch effort to save myself.

"Put up your hands!" he kept yelling. "Put them up or I'll kill you right here. Fight me, you coward."

I kept my hands to my side and continued shaking my head, vowing not to fight. Suddenly Shawn turned and flung the knife into the toilet. Then, with speed and fury, he swung his fists toward my head and chest, barely missing. Thinking I was about to be dismembered, I crouched in my corner, waiting. But to my surprise, Shawn stopped, shook his head in disgust, and walked out a door I thought had been locked. Slamming it again, he left me shaking and cowering in the corner. Already on my knees and thoroughly humiliated, I knelt and thanked God over and over. I had brought this whole thing on myself, but yet again, God delivered me when I called. I had learned a valuable lesson: Keep my mouth shut and eyes on Christ. New in this prison world, I quickly discovered that, unlike in my previous environment, this world didn't revolve around me. I had lost all respect from others in the tank because I didn't fight Shawn. I lost my seat at the tables and now sat on the floor with the fish. This experience would be the first of many humblings God would use to mold and shape my new character.

Finally, after about three months of court appearances, attorney visits, and hearings, I was on my way to getting a trial date set. Already the courtroom was packed, hot, and stuffy. My lawyer looked great in his expensive suit and flashy smile, and I felt confidant things would go my way. But that feeling instantly evaporated upon seeing the same two men sitting silently in the same corner, watching intently. *Those Orange County detectives resemble leopards,* I thought, *stalking me silently.* I could think only of the words "death penalty, death penalty."

A voice intoning, "In the case of Fleck versus the State of California . . ." returned my attention to the front of the courtroom. My lawyer stood and approached the defense table, but unexpectedly the judge called him and the prosecutor to approach the bench. With raised eyebrows and a surprised look, my lawyer strode to the judge's bench. Covering the microphone with his hand, the judge leaned forward as the district attorney began talking to my lawyer. The three conversed in muted tones for a couple of minutes. Then, nodding politely to each other, they turned.

My lawyer walked over to me and pulled me to a secluded spot. "They want to offer you a deal," he began. I smiled, getting butterflies in my stomach thinking of the previous time my lawyer told me we were being offered a deal. That time I had walked out a free man. He continued, "If we go to trial and lose, you could get seven years, and I'm not sure we'd win if we did take your case to trial. They've got a lot of evidence against you—plus this isn't the first time you've been in trouble."

My heart sank at the thought of seven years. No way could I do seven years. "No, no, no." I began to get angry and said, "What am I paying you for? Thirty thousand bucks gets me seven years?" The words hung on the air as a couple of people close by glanced our way. My lawyer looked exasperated that I'd spout off without letting him finish.

"Listen! And listen closely," he growled. "They've offered you sixteen months state prison time; and with the possibility of good-time credit if you don't screw up, you'd do only ten months and twenty days." He finished and stared intently at me.

"Wow. Ten months, twenty days, just about a year," I thought out loud.

"Look," he started back in, "if you don't take this deal, you're an idiot. This is a no-brainer; it doesn't get better than this."

Easy for him to say, I thought silently, weighing the pros and cons and imagining prison life for a "fish" like me. Stories of raping, killing, rioting all clouded my thoughts, and in the back of my mind I believed Clavo and his crew could find me in prison and silence a potential witness to a terrible event. "Mike, can I think about it for a few days?" I begged.

"Nope, it's on the table. Take it now, or we're going to trial next week." Whispering a silent prayer, I paused another few minutes as Mike stayed, waiting impatiently for my response.

Finally I nodded and said, "OK." Feeling defeated, I signed the papers and left the courtroom. Sixteen months. The thought of taking a year out of my life devastated me. How could I do it? A long list of fun things came to mind, and I then wondered what life would be like without them. No going out for pizza, no golfing, no money, no dating, no driving—the list went on. I felt as if I were getting buckled into a roller coaster, watching the bar drop over my lap, feeling the quick jerk of the chains, then the sound of the click, click, clicking, climbing steeply, soon to plummet down the tracks into mind-blowing uncertainty. Fear and anxiety and Clavo's haunting voice made me silently tremble. Satan attacked, but little by little it became easier to fall to my knees and cry out to Jesus.

One morning after a few weeks had passed, the guard came by and said, "Fleck, roll up your stuff. You're 'catching the chain' " (prison jargon for being transferred).

The butterflies jumped into full flight as I nervously packed my few books and toiletries. In the early days inmates were handcuffed, leg-ironed, attached to a long chain at four-foot intervals, and then marched off to their work assignments. Thus the term *chain gang.* Little has changed. Still cuffed and leg-ironed, now we were put on a bus and transferred from county jail to prison, where things get a lot more serious.

For me, sixteen months seemed only slightly short of a lifetime, but it's actually the shortest prison commitment given. First stop on the way to prison is the reception center, a prison used only to classify and determine the final destination of inmates. Newly convicted, it didn't take me long to notice a different world at the reception center. These guards had guns, and they were stationed overhead at every corner, eyeing us intently as a hawk watches a field mouse.

After clearing the front gate, our bus crept to a standstill in front of Receiving and Releasing (R & R). One by one we shuffled down the narrow aisle with leg shackles and handcuffs digging deep, but nobody spoke. At this time it not only would have been futile, but it would have shown weakness. After we had lined up single file, guards unhooked our fetters and, to my disgust, gave the order to disrobe. In unison thirty-five men dropped every stitch of clothing and stood waiting to walk through a metal detector. Humiliated and degraded, one at a time each man passed through, receiving smug smirks from the calloused staff. Finally the ordeal ended inside the R & R with the officer handing us our "fish rolls," which contained bedding and an issue of T-shirts and boxers.

I struggled to take in the new surroundings. It seemed so long ago when I rode my horse with my dad or played with my dog on the warm front porch of our farmhouse. *What happened? Where did that innocence go?* A glance at the deep marks inflicted by my cuffs jarred me back to the present.

I spent two months in reception being classified and then assigned to Chuckawalla Valley State Prison (CVSP). During another long bus ride, more nostalgia filled my mind as I sat watching the outside world pass by only inches away. With the steel cuffs once again cutting my wrists and ankles, I watched car after car pass by as I wondered how long until I would be free and could roll *my* window down and feel the rush of air blast through *my* hair. I saw things I had never noticed before: the little shrubs beside the road, the beautiful palm trees lining housing developments, the cloud shadows moving over the hills. I seemed to be seeing the world for the first time, and I hoped to see it again someday.

Chapter 18

CHUCKAWALLA VALLEY
STATE PRISON

The desert had never looked so beautiful as we left it behind, turning off the freeway onto a long, lonely road. Razor wire topped the chain link fence that surrounded the almost windowless buildings. Gun towers every three hundred yards sat motionless like enormous brutes with beady eyes watching, waiting to strike.

I felt terror as our bus rolled through the gate. After we exited the bus, guards herded us into holding cells and gave us our state issue of clothing. I found it so hard to grasp that only a few months before, I had more clothes than two closets could hold, but now all that I had to my name lay neatly folded in my lap.

Chuckawalla Valley State Prison, located near the small town of Blythe, sits near the Arizona border. Desert on every side makes it unlikely for anyone to survive even if escape were possible. Prisoners share stories of men escaping only to be found dead or near-dead from exposure and dehydration. Arriving in May, I was unaware of, but would soon learn about, the sweltering summer heat. After receiving my housing number and bed assignment, I found myself sitting on a bunk staring at a bunch of unfamiliar and scary faces. Although the building roared with activity, I wanted only to curl up on my bunk and pretend I wasn't there.

A medium-security facility, Chuckawalla has little serious violence, but I felt threatened and scared. The housing units are huge, and the safety of my little county jail tank was gone. Instead of two dozen guys, up to two hundred fifty men roamed freely through a giant dayroom. In contrast to single cells, side-by-side bunks were crammed together in a two-tier open dormitory, and shower blocks with rows of steaming nozzles replaced single stalls. The dormitory was never still. Like a stirring anthill, it pulsed day and night.

Each night I prayed God would keep me safe and direct me to some like-minded Christians to hang out with. As always, my Lord and Savior answered quickly. One evening, while strolling through the dayroom, I noticed four guys sitting at a table. Instead of dominoes, cards, or food, they had Bibles spread open. *Jackpot! Thank You, Lord!*

I introduced myself and from that day on I spent each evening at the table praying and studying God's Word. At first I felt totally out of place, and my old self longed to be sitting with the big group, being one of the "in" guys. All the sideways looks and second glances of passersby made me nervous. But before long, those feelings died, and I knew I had found a home with my brothers.

Basically, I had little faith and only a beginning understanding of Christianity. It was one thing to tell my family a thousand miles away that I had become a Christian, but quite another to begin a walk worthy of the name. I had started smoking again, but now it didn't satisfy as before. Yes, I prayed often that God would relieve me of the habit, but I continued to smoke.

Finding a job is one of the most important tasks upon arriving in prison because having an assigned job changes everything. With a job come privileges—using the phone goes from once a month to daily, if so desired; canteen purchases go from fifty dollars a month to a hundred forty dollars, if an inmate can afford it; but most important, a job brings with it the sought-after "good time" credit, which turns a sixteen-month sentence into ten months and twenty days. Also known as one-third time, it means that whatever the sentence, it gets cut by a third, provided the inmate doesn't get into trouble. So from day one I solicited every guard and free staff I could find, hoping to land a job, but nothing materialized.

A month after I arrived at Chuckawalla, my parents came to visit. Feeling like a teenager on his first date, I wanted to look good for them. Our previous visit had been in the county jail, where we talked on a telephone through thick glass for only a fifty-five-minute visit. In contrast, here we met in a large room with tables, vending machines, and a large outdoor patio shaded with big umbrellas. Visiting hours lasted from 9:00 A.M. until 3:00 P.M. Friday to Sunday, giving lots of time with loved ones. The best part of our visit was finally hugging and touching my parents. I acted like an octopus that day, enjoying their affection. With no physical contact allowed in prison for obvious reasons, I found my body starving for affection. Hugs were truly therapeutic.

Our visits started and ended in tears, and the three days seemed like three minutes, leaving me with a heart-wrenching loneliness as I watched them disappear behind the exit doors. Bleeding tears internally but only misting outwardly, I returned to the other world I called home. Putting on a front is the only way to avoid the parasites that feed on others' pain, because showing pain or fear inevitably brings the wrath of those who love to exploit others.

Writing became my way of crying, of questioning, and of rejoicing. I read and wrote voraciously; it seemed I couldn't get enough information on spiritual subjects and how to live a Christian life.

A couple of days later, still missing my parents and feeling as if the visit opened a new wound instead of opening an old one, I wrote:

Dear Mom and Dad,

Well, it was hard leaving the visiting room the other day. I felt as if I were turning my back on life itself. You two are so strong and forgiving and supportive that I just thank God for parents like you. It's hard to be in prison clothes seeing you guys in street clothes and knowing that you live where things are so innocent, and you don't have to be constantly on guard and in stress involving life and death. When I got back to my bed, my eyes got misty and my heart was heavy. I love you guys more than you know! Well, I better talk about something else before I lose it for good!

I am still dreaming about camp meeting . . . someday I'll tell my story to people—you watch! I have *The Desire of Ages* and a Venden book—thanks a lot! I still don't have a job and cannot understand why. I've prayed fervently and still no action. Guess God has a reason for not wanting me busy. Maybe He figures that the more time I have to spare, the more I can learn by reading. That's pretty much all I do—sweat, eat, sweat, workout, sweat, read, sweat, sleep, and, of course, sweat! It's 126 degrees!

Time here is so good/bad/happy/sad—just like a roller coaster. But the best part is, no one can stop the clock! I'll be home soon. I love you.

God bless, Rick

Did I really believe the horrible events in Orange County would simply disappear? Or was I offering them hope but only fooling myself?

Chapter 19

EXPECTING
PAROLE

I'll be home soon." Funny how I naively thought my wicked past would just fade away. God's plan for me had just started; the roller coaster hadn't even begun its first descent. I'm glad God buckled me tightly because this ride soon became bumpy. Satan initiated a new series of attempts to derail my fresh start with God in my life. When I discovered that my first bunkie was a self-proclaimed satanist, I thought to myself, *This is just perfect. Why would God put a man who openly holds services to Satan so close to me, knowing that only a few months ago I, too, openly served Satan?*

Waking early in the morning, I'd quietly open the Word and, still learning to pray, I'd ask for every conceivable blessing, some I perhaps should not have prayed to receive. But being sure that God really existed, I knew He'd make that decision. Often my bunkie said things to discourage me such as, "If there's a God, why did He let you end up here?" I tried to defend myself but usually failed miserably. Then one day I noticed a giant new upside-down pentagram painted on the door of his locker. I shook my head and asked, "What's the deal with that?"

Laughing, he replied, "I fight fire with fire!" The symbol reminded me of the many times I'd held secret worship meetings with Satan, and I, too, had sketched and drawn many satanic symbols including the common upside-down pentagram. Drugs of all kinds were abundant, and often I saw men huddled around a bunk with a couple of them "keeping point" or watching for the floor cops who made their rounds occasionally. Watching inmates passing around an old dirty needle made me sick with memories I desperately wanted to forget. At times like this, the desire to use returned, driving me to my knees begging my Savior for relief.

One night, several hours after I'd fallen asleep, a light tapping on my shoulder awakened me. Startled, I jerked my head up with my eyes wide open trying to focus in the dim light. The silhouette of my bunkie hovering over me did not present a welcome sight and ordinarily would have caused a train of verbiage only a lumberjack could appreciate. But when he spoke, my attitude changed.

"Hey, Homie, sorry to wake you," he began in a frightened whisper. "You have to help me out. I need you to do me a favor."

Awake now and sitting up on my bunk, I rubbed my eyes to clear the cobwebs of sleep. "What's the problem?"

"They're coming to get me. I heard them talking, and they're going to bust me. I need you to do me a favor quick—no time to waste. Please, here, go ahead, no, it . . . Quick, hurry, they're on to me. . . ."

He talked so fast that I couldn't even make out some of his words. He kept repeating himself, sounding more frightened each second. Pushing a small round container into my chest, he begged me to get rid of the contents. Opening the lid, I smelled methamphetamine, which instantly made my mouth water and my body tremble. The smell and sight, coupled with the nonstop rambling of my paranoid bunkie, presented a crushing temptation to use. Immediately I said, "No!" But I didn't hand the container back to him.

Time slowed as I gazed at the euphoria sitting in my hands. Then slowly I finally handed the container back saying firmly, "No, I won't do it. I'm sorry."

Quickly taking the container, he began pacing and looking for a place to hide it, and I rolled over and prayed that he'd not hide it in my bunk space or locker. He'd been using speed for a couple of days, and finally the lack of sleep had sprung a paranoia that the cops were going to bust him. Unable to sleep, I lay for the next few hours talking silently to God about how I understood I'd be tested but didn't know if I could resist another temptation like that. I'd never before been that close to my favorite drug and not used it; it was exhilarating yet frightening to experience God's strength so obviously imparted to me. Being an addict for so many years, I'd never before felt the unmistakable power of God by using the word *No!* It always had been *Yes*, even if I knew I shouldn't use. But this time something supernatural, a power not of my own, stopped me, and in the days following, I felt strengthened by the victory of that night.

Summer came with the heat of the desert withering even the sturdiest convict. We watered the steel bars on the weight pile so our hands wouldn't burn as we did our daily workouts.

Still job hunting, I heard of an opening in the laundry department, so I quickly ran to check with the supervisor. A month earlier I'd spoken to him about another opening that eventually fell through. He remembered me and said I had an excellent chance this time. Excited at the prospect, I thanked God and started back toward my building. Passing the education department, something told me to go inside. After walking through the door, I strolled to the front desk where one of the teachers sat. "I'm looking for a clerk's job. Do you have any openings?" I asked.

Looking up and removing her glasses, she smiled apologetically shaking her head. "No, I'm sorry, I don't. Oh—wait a minute." Putting her glasses back on, she picked up a phone and dialed a number. "Uh huh. Oh—there is? OK, I'll bring him in." As she came around the desk, she said, "You're in luck. What's your name, sir?"

"Fleck," I replied excitedly.

"A clerk's job just opened today," she said over her shoulder. "Follow me."

We walked down a sterile hall with classrooms on both sides. As we turned the corner, I saw two teachers talking in front of what appeared to be a private office. I recognized one man as the one I'd spoken to a month before about a job. He looked at me and smiled. "Hey, you're back."

Then turning to the female teacher, he explained how I had almost gotten the previous clerk's job. And he thought I'd be an excellent worker. *With this recommendation, how can I miss?* I wondered to myself. Smiling from ear to ear, I nodded as the female teacher told me to come back the next day.

Once back in my building, I sat on my bunk weighing the odds. I'd probably have to take a typing test, and although I'm no hotshot, I could type a letter. Twenty years earlier, I'd taken Typing 10 as a sophomore in high school, never dreaming how the training would help me. But a problem loomed. I had only three months of prison time left to do, and supervisors generally hire people with more time so they don't have to train and then retrain. Pondering the options, I figured one of the two had to be mine. Later that night a guy I knew came to me beaming. "Look—I got it. I got the job!" There he stood holding his little white job ducat.

I grabbed it and read, "Inmate Laundry Assignment." I was steamed! I faked a smile and said, "Good for you." Now my options were cut in half—clerk or nothing. Working in the education department as a teacher's clerk is a prized job. This department was one of only a handful lucky enough to have air-conditioning; in addition, it paid more because a high-school diploma was required. Pay started at eleven cents an hour. Yes, eleven cents.

Don't be too quick to laugh—many jobs have no pay. One is called the rock crew—two guys, one shovel, and a wheelbarrow. Oh, did I forget to mention a forty-foot-high pile of rocks? Several teams would head off the yard after breakfast to the giant pile located on one side of the vast prison grounds.

Chuckawalla has four full yards called facilities. Each one has a perimeter fence separating it from the others and a massive, lethal electric fence with manned gun towers surrounding all four facilities and separating us from society. The rock pile sits on the outer limits. Inmates grumblingly fill the wheelbarrows and march single file to the opposite side of the huge prison, where they unload the rocks onto a portable conveyer belt taking them up forty feet and dropping them, starting the next pile. When all the rocks are moved, the whole process repeats itself as crews move them back. The rock crews gave me lots of incentive to find a good job. I didn't want to be stuck moving rocks!

Eleven cents an hour truly is peanuts, but at the end of the month, twenty dollars can buy some toiletries or snacks, which many never see. The state supplies soap, razors, toilet paper, toothbrush, and tooth powder (usually used to scrub the sink—works great!). But it's always nice to be able to buy a few treats. I thank God daily for the support, both emotionally and financially, my parents and others gave me, but I felt guilty coming from the canteen loaded with food and goodies while others looked on knowing they'd not be shopping anytime soon.

The next morning at 9:00 A.M., I entered the education department. Finding the classroom, I strolled in nervously, expecting to see three or four others waiting to take the clerk's test. But to my surprise, only the teacher was present. "Good morning, Mr. Fleck." I nodded and smiled, sitting at a desk in front of her. With no typewriter in sight, I wondered what was going on. Closing the book she was reading, she looked up and asked, "Do you have high school GED?"

"Absolutely!" I replied and then went on to stretch the truth by adding, "I also have two years of college." (Two years of attending college succeeding only in drunken debauchery.)

Looking impressed, she said, "OK then, you'll start Friday. Let me get your number and housing location before you go, and when you come back, bring a book or two. You'll have plenty of spare time." I walked out with my feet barely touching the floor.

"Thank You, Jesus!" My heart rejoiced in thankfulness. I reported to work Friday morning carrying a copy of *Patriarchs and Prophets,* the perfect read. I loved that book and found it hard to put down.

At work I wrote a letter to a friend telling him I forgave him for what he did to me. Just seven months earlier, I would like to have caught him alone. But now, thanks to my new heart transplant, the Holy Spirit convicted me to continue making many wrongs right. After experiencing the forgiveness of our Father in heaven and knowing that He sent His Son to die for us even though we continue to fall short—how could I justify holding a grudge?

I enjoyed my new job and pleasant boss, especially knowing that I could now qualify for the "good time" credits, which established my parole date, October 10, 1994, just over three months away. Each morning I went to work one day closer to freedom. You would have had to look long and hard to catch me without a smile on my face.

That changed one fateful day only a couple weeks after I had started to work. At lunchtime while I sat on the grass outside the education department, I heard my name ringing over the yard loudspeaker. "Fleck, report to the program officer immediately."

Startled, I rose, went to the row of offices and gave my ID to the guard who motioned me to the lieutenant's office. "Sit down, Fleck," the gruff voice of a hard-looking, older lieutenant barked.

I sat and stared apprehensively back at him. Just then two other guards walked in and began eyeing me like a fresh steak— the insignia on their uniforms told me they were part of an inter-prison investigation unit known as ISU, a group nobody wanted to see under any circumstances. Immediately I suspected the worst. *What did they find? Did my bunkie plant something in my locker? Drugs? Oh no, I'm only three months from getting out. What's happening?*

Finally the lieutenant spoke. "So, Fleck, what do you know about a double murder in Orange County?"

His words hit me like a cold piece of steel slicing through my mind. My mouth went dry. I felt nauseated. Staring blankly back, saying nothing, I began to sweat and shiver at the same time. *Oh, please, Lord, don't let this happen to me.* My words silently went to the throne, but God's answer wasn't favorable that day. "I . . . I . . . don't have anything to say," I finally stammered looking into their eyes hoping this was a mistake.

"Stand up, turn around, put your hands behind your back, Fleck," one of the guards ordered as he pulled a pair of handcuffs from his vest.

"What are you doing?" I asked.

"You're being placed in administrative segregation due to an impending murder investigation in Orange County," he replied coldly.

"Ad seg?" The words hung in the air. "Isn't that 'the hole'?" I questioned as he escorted me out of the office and onto the yard.

"Yep," he said. Everyone on the yard watched and wondered what I'd done as he led me out through the gates. In an instant my whole world had collapsed. Once in ad seg, officers stripped me, searched me, gave me a jumpsuit, and escorted me to an empty, dark, humid cell. I walked to the edge of the bunk, knelt down, and began to cry. I sobbed uncontrollably for a while until my knees began to hurt. Crawling onto the hard bunk, eyes blurred with tears, I lay motionless, staring at nothing.

Ad seg is a depressing place, a place used to house inmates who have violated prison policy in any one of many ways. I was now in violation because a murder suspect cannot be housed in a medium-security facility. Orange County had placed a "parole hold" on me, stating I was a suspect in a homicide case. Orange County's hold caused the administration at Chuckawalla to take me off the main line and into a maximum-security unit waiting for formal charges. I had only three months before parole, and this would be my home until then. The Orange County district attorney hadn't formally filed charges yet, so I hoped that they'd not have enough evidence to charge me and that I would be released.

My emotional roller coaster intensified in ad seg. It seemed that my life had been turned upside down. While serving my sentence, I had focused on my parole date and had tried to put the potential murder charges out of my mind by rationalizing that maybe the detectives had figured out everything and decided I was neither the problem nor the solution. I felt devastated to be pulled from my job, tossed into ad seg, and told that I was being charged with a double homicide. Then I'd feel peace after I spent time really talking with God and rededicating my life daily. I acknowledged He was in control.

When I was stressed, it was not about my long-term eternal future; it was just about the short term. I asked God why things had to be so difficult. Then I would remember what I had read—the path to heaven is rough, narrow, and treacherous; the journey is long and hard. I understood that it really doesn't matter about this life here; it's eternal life that counts. But I had some short-term dreams I wanted to pursue when I was released. All of them had to do with helping people. I dreamed that Rod, my brother, and I could go to school together. I thought about studying theology or medicine. I'd also dream of ways to preach the Word when released and wrote my parents of my decision. I told them I had confirmed my life with God and decided once and for all to do His will no matter what lay ahead. I hoped to work in some kind of ministry or evangelistic outreach for teens, preteens, and adults, although I'd see God's will for my life more clearly when paroled. I could also imagine myself as a social worker, dealing with kids off the street or just out of juvenile detention centers.

I believed God would never let me starve, but I didn't want to think about getting rich again until God gave me the ability to handle money and the motivation to succeed. I had no drive to earn a dime; my mind wasn't thinking dollars at all, and I felt that I grew more each day because of the no-stress-over-money factor. But I had a different worry—a serious need to "let-go-and-let-God." I asked God to show me into the future, just a little to put my mind at ease. He didn't! He said He wanted me to trust Him with everything—mind, body, soul—so that in the next part of my life when I would tell somebody of conviction, I wouldn't just tell it, I'd live it.

Somewhere along the line an inmate gave me the nickname "Skip," which stuck like glue. Many inmates have nicknames, and often when I looked at an individual and then learned his nickname, I immediately understood the connection. For instance: "Fingers," a small man with a birth defect leaving him with what looked like two fistfuls of thumbs with no third joint; "Face," one of the most hideous-looking men I'd seen, but he always managed a mangled yet friendly smile; "Droopy," an inmate with eyes that sagged almost to the point of oddity; "One-ton," 360 pounds and five feet six inches. Need I say more? "Wicked," "Lefty," "Smiley," "Smokey," "Cowboy," "Knuckles," and many, many variations of each of the seven dwarfs—the list goes on. So my name became Skip, an unassuming, harmless name that I accepted and adopted.

My days in the hole began to show signs of sunlight as God prepared my path through the knowledge of His Word.

After a few weeks alone, I was happy when the door opened and a celly walked in, the first of many. Although I felt unsure what to say, I knew God would guide me. But like every new Christian, I stumbled over myself when trying to explain the supernatural change of being born again. Trial and error and trusting the Spirit's discernment takes awhile.

I casually had known my new celly before. He'd been in prison nine out of his last eleven years and was well adjusted to the system. Only twenty-four, he took his first commitment as a juvenile for attempted murder and did three years out of nine on that charge. Some guy had raped his sister, he shot him, the guy lived, but my celly had been back and forth ever since. When I asked what he planned to do when he got out this time, he said, "Dope." Sadly, he was already headed back to prison, and he hadn't even left yet—it's too bad but there was not much I could do for him except pray. Once I started to mention a bit about the Bible, but he cut me short: "I don't believe in God or mess around with religion." So I dropped the subject and prayed that some other time he would be receptive.

I doubted the district attorney would file and still thought I'd be going home soon, so I told my folks to plan that I'd be released on the tenth. If anything changed, then I'd deal with it, but for now I trusted that God would allow me to be released from hell and go on to my new life with Him. I loved God and tried to make Him the center of my life.

With my parole date only two days away and seeing no sign of the formal arrest warrant from Orange County, that night I thanked God for delivering me from this horrible place and the possibility of a murder trial. I fell asleep confident my prayers would be answered. Having pleaded numerous times for a glimpse into the future, I eventually saw the wisdom of God in denying those petitions.

Chapter 20

PENAL CODE NUMBER 187—MURDER CHARGE

The next morning started with a beautiful sunrise accompanied by a warm tray of prison breakfast and ice-cold milk. The closer I came to my parole date, the more excited I became. Lying on my bunk for what seemed minutes but soon turned to hours, I dreamed of the first, second, and third things I planned to do during the first minutes of freedom. People say "single digit midgets" (inmates with nine days or less until parole) crawl the walls with anticipation and anxiety and have sleepless nights and painfully slow days. I can vouch for the feeling that only a convict can understand as he counts down the days until freedom becomes reality.

On Saturday I spent the day relaxing and reading some good things in my Bible. I hoped the authorities would come get me soon. I wanted my freedom and new life and waited for it anxiously. But my daydreaming came to a devastating end when the counselor gave me an arrest warrant about noon on Sunday. I was bummed out to say the least; I had planned to get out Monday and just leave the entire bad dream behind. So I cried and felt sorry for myself until evening. I wrote two letters, and then the guards came to my cell and said I was moving. But when I got settled in my new cell and looked out the window to watch a beautiful sunset, I felt a flood of good emotions—relief and peace in my heart. God was leading me and wanted total control. I just needed to relax and sit back and watch. I made up my mind that each day of my life would be dedicated to trying to talk to someone about Christ. Each day just one word, one sentence, or at least the consciousness of spreading the faith at all times, so when there was an opportunity, I wouldn't miss it. The county jail is prime location for talking to people about Christ, and I didn't want to miss a lick!

I reasoned that this warrant and move had to happen so my innocence could be proved completely and nothing could ever stop me from doing God's work. I felt happy to have everything resolved while still confined rather than having a taste of freedom and then having it taken away. I thought this setback also gave my interstate parole stuff time to clear so I could go straight to Andrews University when the trial ended, if that was God's plan.

I sensed my parents' disappointment and could understand it. I felt truly sorry and prayed that God would give them the peace of mind He had given me. I wrote them, "Don't worry. He will provide for my spiritual and mental needs if you guys can give me a hand with physical and moral needs. Deal? Thanks. I love you guys."

Writing had become my only avenue of processing my thoughts because prison taught me to keep things to myself and discuss problems with no one. But with such crushing news, I had to tell someone, and now I found that the parents I had lied to, disappointed, and shunned were my best friends. I could now tell them everything, and for the first time in many years, I could see their wisdom—wisdom I mistook for control and fanaticism in my rebellious years. I marveled at their ability to find the silver lining, look to God for guidance, and show me unconditional love. These attributes always had been there—why hadn't I seen them before?

I spent most of the night in prayer mixed with a little sleep. I'd awake, cry, pray, and then doze off and then repeat the cycle. The next morning, right after breakfast, two guards appeared at my door. "Fleck, are you ready?" they asked.

Having barely slept and eaten little, I said, "Let's go." The cool fall morning with mingled smells of sage and fresh cut grass tickled my nose, and the already bright sun made me squint, trying to take in the prison surroundings one last time. After a series of questions to verify I was Rick Fleck, the control gate opened to the holding cell where inmates ready to parole waited. A handful of guys with nervous smiles and new clothes sent by their families waited anxiously for the freedom-bringing moment. Whites joked with Blacks, Blacks joked with Mexicans, the racial lines obliterated by one thing in common—going home.

The sergeant entered, and after getting everyone's signature, one by one he passed out "gate money," two hundred dollars minus bus fare, to all except me. "Fleck, you ain't going home today. Orange County's coming for you. I'll give your money to them." I already knew this, and his gruff, matter-of-fact voice only added to my sadness. Wanting desperately to feel the anticipation and joy this handful of men were feeling, I stared at their faces and watched every expression, hoping to lift my own spirits.

"OK, Gentlemen, the van is here. Go, and don't come back," the sergeant shouted with a look of sarcasm. The room emptied and with them went all their cheer and excitement, leaving me staring at the cement walls and choking back tears. Moments later the door opened again, and a bad situation was only made worse by what I saw. Two menacing, cold faces appeared, each wearing his own intimidating smirk. Wrist and ankle cuffs in hand, they crossed the cell floor stopping only inches from me. Then, as if in a rerun of a bad-cop movie, one of them recited the very words he had spat in my face ten months earlier. "Remember us?" he said with a cool whisper, as the smell of spearmint gum filled my nostrils. My knees shook. "What did I tell you, Fleck? I told you we'd get you, didn't I? Didn't I?"

Saying nothing, I tried not to show my fear but failed miserably as I put my shaking hands up to accept the handcuffs. "Turn around, Fleck, and kneel down," he spat as he fastened the ankle cuffs tightly. Like a chained animal, head hung low, I shuffled out through the morning air and into a waiting unmarked police car. The giant gates closed behind us, and Chuckawalla Valley State Prison shrank in the distance. One detective had taken the adjacent backseat with me, and I knew this would be a trying four-hour trip back to Orange County.

"Are you comfortable?" he asked, staring at me and chewing his gum methodically. I nodded, saying nothing. My mind raced; I'd never felt so uncomfortable in all my life. I knew what they wanted and braced myself for the interrogation attack sure to follow the insincere pleasantries. As soon as we hit the freeway, it began.

"Fleck, we already know what happened," he began in a calm, serious voice. "We have Clavo in custody, along with your other accomplice, and they've been very cooperative in filling in the events of that night." My mouth went dry, and I tried to breathe evenly. "They've given us all the information we need to make sure you will die by lethal injection. . . ." His words hung in the air. I was feeling chilled. Had they turned the air-conditioning on?

"Fleck, we've heard you're a Christian now. Do you think God's going to save you after what you did? You executed two people, Fleck. Nobody can save you. You're going to die." He sat back, letting the weight of his words push me even deeper into depression. "Fleck, do you want your family to watch you die?"

For the first time I turned and looked at him but said nothing. He noticed my reaction and continued, but now in an almost consoling way. "Look, Rick—it's Rick, isn't it?" I nodded. He continued, "Your accomplices have implicated you as the shooter, but we don't think it went exactly like that." He paused and glanced at the rearview mirror, which I noticed had been aimed so his partner could watch me while he drove. I could feel the noose being tightened.

"We have the other two in custody, and we know there were three of you. They've told us this, but you can save your life now by telling us exactly what happened that night." He threw out the bait and sat back staring intently at me.

Instantly I knew they were lying—why did they need anything from me if they already had the whole story from my co-defendants? They'd said, "The other two," but I knew that three went into the trailer, and none of them were me.

I whispered a silent prayer for strength and decided not to play the game. "So," I began, "do you guys golf?" They looked at each other, then back at me.

"Fleck, do you want to help yourself or not?" one of them spat back.

With my head turned toward the window, I said, "I like golf, or at least I used to. Great game to relieve stress, get exercise. Do you guys exercise? Probably so, don't you? I started working out in prison. Really feels good. I also started studying my Bible." This time I turned and looked directly at my interrogator. "Do you believe in God?" I asked seriously.

He slumped back into his seat, signaling game over for a while. We drove along silently for a while listening to the tires. I thanked God for His strength and pleaded with Him to keep me safe from Clavo who, I assumed, had been told the same lies about me. But whether Clavo would believe them or not, remained to be seen.

After a while, the interrogation resumed. Both detectives took their turn at manipulative questions, hoping to extract information. I sat quietly, head turned to the passing countryside, praying to my Lord and Comforter. Four hours later, the trip ended, but not until the driver purposely detoured past the scene of the crime of that awful night. They watched me intently as they crept past the vacant trailer and sight of such horror. I again felt nauseated but said nothing.

A few hours later, after fingerprinting, photographing, and general booking procedures, I sat by myself in another filthy holding cell waiting for housing. But this time I really wasn't alone. My Savior had sent His Spirit and holy angels to comfort me. Along with a Bible I had persuaded the guards to let me keep, I was ready for whatever tomorrow had to give or take.

The next day I walked into the Orange County Jail system, and with a bedroll on my shoulder and Bible under my arm, I entered my new mission field, young in the faith but filled with anticipation. The last three months of solitary confinement in ad seg had armed me with Scripture and strength in Christ Jesus.

Chapter 21

FACING THE
DEATH PENALTY

*W*ill Clavo try to silence me? Am I going to make it out alive? Will I get the death penalty? These and similar questions caused me to make a daily and sometimes hourly commitment to God, asking Him to protect me and give me strength.

At the same time, I sometimes found myself questioning His will and often trying to blame Him for this obviously mistaken murder charge. *Lord, You know I now serve You. You know I didn't kill those people, so why am I here, and what are You going to do about it?* A constant battle between trust and doubt raged in my mind. Only by opening my Bible and reading my beloved Savior's promises over and over did I receive peace.

I quickly discovered a large group of Christians housed in the jail. As always, men hoping to win their cases were willing to try anything to help avoid convictions. Many turn to religion and, during the time in jail fighting their charges, they seem dedicated to following Jesus. Sadly, when their trial arrived and they would learn the often-disastrous outcome, they would then abandon their Bibles and their Christian claims when they entered prison. While determined not to be one of these men, still in the quiet time of the early morning hours when my mind wouldn't allow my body to sleep, I wondered how I would accept the outcome of my trial?

After a few days officials escorted me to court and arraigned me on double homicide charges with special circumstances. A nicely dressed middle-aged woman holding a bundle of papers approached me, and looking over her bifocals, said, "Are you Richard Fleck?"

I smiled and said, "Yes, Ma'am, I am."

Her smile turned to a woeful look of pity as she slowly shook her head and replied, "You're so young."

Taken aback, I must have looked questioningly at her. So she continued, "You, you know what you're charged with, don't you?"

Still saying nothing, my eyes must have revealed that I had little clue what was going on.

"Mr. Fleck, you're facing the death penalty. I suggest you find a good lawyer."

Death penalty, death penalty. The words chilled my soul. Watching her walk away, I wondered what she saw when she looked at me. Did she see a vicious killer or a scared young man completely out of his element?

An old gentleman reached through the bars and offered his hand to me, jarring me back to reality. "Hi, I'm James Enright. I'll be representing you." Astonished but happy, I shook it vigorously, eying him up and down, seeing a man dressed in average clothes, nothing too confident about him at all.

"So this is him, huh, God?" I whispered silently, not convinced but sure of God's choice. My last lawyer and this guy were about as opposite as the difference between steak and Spam®. The first leaves you full and confident; the latter makes you wonder if you even wanted to bother eating. As I came to realize over the next three and a half years, people get what they pay for.

Jim Enright, the state-appointed attorney, was all I had now that my bank account was depleted. *But,* I asked myself, *does*

God need a high-priced flashy lawyer to accomplish His will? Of course not! Actually, it'll be more amazing when an attorney of this caliber proves my innocence and sets me free.

So, with this assurance, I set out to do the work God had prepared for me while here. The Orange County Jail system has top-notch worship programs. Five days a week I could go to services held in the basement chapel. Along with the elderly, dedicated chaplains, various groups came in to sing and preach the Word. I could not have asked for a better experience.

I had hoped to attend school when released from prison, but because release seemed unlikely for some time, I sent for a catalog from the Griggs University distance learning program. I was shocked to learn that tuition for each university class was close to five hundred dollars. My heart sank; I could never afford these classes. I lay back on my bunk and contemplated throwing away the catalog, along with my dreams of college, but something stirred inside of me, and I began to pray: *Dear Lord, You know I'm going to be here awhile. If You would like me to learn more about You, I ask that You supply the funds needed. Not my will but Yours only. Thank You. Amen.* With that I sent a letter to Griggs University explaining my situation and requesting financial aid.

A couple weeks later I ripped open a letter from Griggs University, informing me that I qualified for the worthy-student fund, which reduced the cost by about half. But joy faded as I realized I still couldn't pay the amount needed. So that night I prayed again, thanking God for the portion He'd already covered but asking if He'd cover the rest. Then I wrote another letter thanking them for the discount and asking if they knew anywhere else I could apply for the balance. Week after week passed, and I'd all but given up on the dream of school when a letter arrived with another catalog. Unsure, I opened it, and my eyes bulged when I read the following: "Mr. Fleck, we are happy to inform you an anonymous donor has agreed to pay the remaining amount for your class. Please fill out the proper forms, submit them ASAP, and your course will follow. Thank you."

Before long I had a pile of books and assignments. Really happy to get classes underway, I felt special warmth knowing that these books were a direct answer to *my* prayers. God might have been keeping my faith alive by answering a prayer that kept me busy while waiting for my case to come to court. I saw guys around me every day with lonely, bored expressions on their faces. But God had seen to it that my days were filled with school and writing. God obviously had a plan, and as time went on, it slowly unfolded. I felt structure and discipline beginning to form too. Structure and discipline are of the utmost importance to recovering addicts, so this program proved good in more ways than one. Each day had more education for me.

God is eager to work in everyone's lives, and He never took His hand off my shoulder. He stayed with me always, although I occasionally lost my focus. He knew I needed to come to know Him and trust Him in my own way. My parents and I had to be strong and realize that no matter what happened, He was with us. He had saved me from so much harm, and more and more I could see how He had obviously answered prayers.

He made my time at OCJ as pleasant as possible for me. I knew at times prison life sounded difficult to my parents, especially when I started to feel down and expressed it to them. But I had experienced nothing but love every day since I accepted Jesus as my Savior. So many bad things could have happened in jail, and yet my prayers were answered day in and day out. I continued to dream that when God saw fit, I would walk onto a church platform and tell my story.

Chapter 22

MIRACLE AFTER
MIRACLE

Some days the devil crept back in with his nonstop lies, and often I'd need a pick-me-up miracle to urge me on. God never failed. He was always right on time, giving me just enough to get through the day.

One day I woke up feeling depressed, abandoned, and not at peace. I was definitely focusing on myself. I'd been trying to seek God and ask His help to overcome certain habits that I battled daily. I was struggling with improper thoughts and attitudes and felt a little angry with God that I didn't seem to be gaining victories. Instead of reading my Bible and doing my psychology lessons, I went to the dayroom to play chess with the guys. I felt so guilty because I knew why I wasn't doing my lessons—I was sulking. Then for dinner we had liver—yuk! Never eaten it, never will—another bummer. Instead of going back to the dayroom, I elected to stay at my bunk. I eyed my Bible but grabbed a novel. Immediately a voice said to me, *"Pick up the Word and read."* So I did.

I didn't read anything that got my attention or seemed relevant to my world; in fact, I fell asleep. About 6:00 A.M. I was awakened by someone yelling to the guard asking if he was going to let us go to church. Sleep was so comforting that my response was to slink deeper into my covers and hope the guard wouldn't call us for church. Feeling guilty for choosing to skip church, I tried to shift the responsibility to God. I prayed, *Lord, if You want me to go to church, get me out of bed, dress me, and make me happy.* I figured that was a tall order, and if He did all that, I'd go. I felt fairly safe because that particular guard never committed himself to anything. All of a sudden my door opened! The bars clang noisily, and everyone notices when a door opens. I couldn't figure it out, so I quickly dressed and walked to the front. The cop opened the next gate leading to the hallway, and I asked him, "What's up?"

"It's time for church," he growled.

"The others want to know if they can come too," I answered.

"I know. I heard them." And he walked away.

"OK, God, You made Your point. I'm up and dressed—now make me happy!"

I found my favorite group at church, along with a Southern Baptist guy who used to sing in a country band. It was always enthusiastic and noisy when he sang and preached. Soon I was singing along and even smiling. Returning to my cell happy, peaceful, and focused, I got on my knees and thanked God for being faithful even when I was faithless.

Christian church services were a nice break from the violence and terrible monotony of life inside, so I usually attended them all. Sunday services were my favorite, as the chaplain always brought in an especially good group.

My tank housed fourteen guys. During football season the TV in the dayroom is of more importance than any church service. The deputy in charge knows that, so he doesn't even bother coming to ask if anyone wants to attend. I would have to specifically ask to attend church.

One Sunday my favorite team was playing a vicious rival. The game would be a tooth-and-nail match. These teams probably wouldn't meet again that season, and I really wanted to see the game. And it was Sunday, not Sabbath. I had attended church the previous Sunday, Monday, Tuesday, and Thursday, as well as having my private service on Sabbath. I really wanted to see this game. *Can't I skip it just this once?* I rationalized, hoping for a big *Yeah, go ahead.*

The time for the service came closer and closer. Because I hadn't let the deputy know I wanted to attend, I knew he wouldn't come open the door. And in jail, there is no such thing as going a little late.

I sat in the dayroom watching the coin toss as the teams did their final warm-ups in anticipation of a knock-down, drag-out game. At that instant I decided not to ask the deputy to open the gate. *I'll just skip it this one time. No big deal,* I rationalized.

Halfway through the first quarter, the gate opened and the deputy called my name over the intercom and told me to report to the deputy station. My mind raced. *What have I done?* A trip to the station is not something to look forward to.

As I approached the station, the main gate to the hallway clanged open, and I stepped into the vestibule. "What's the problem?" I asked the deputy.

"Time for church. Go to the hallway and line up," he growled before turning on his heel and walking away.

I was shocked. This had never happened before. I hadn't asked to go to church. The deputy hadn't asked if I wanted to go to church; he told me to go! *OK, it's church.* I shrugged and went down the hallway. At the beautiful service I received a blessing like a breath of cool fresh air in the middle of a hot, humid day.

After the service, I paused in the vestibule leading to my tank, waiting for the gate to open and thinking about watching the end of the game. At that instant the gate opened, and as I entered the dayroom, my knees almost buckled. In the middle of the room lay one of the new inmates, stripped to his boxers and blood running down his face. A second inmate was in even worse shape. The game on TV played in an otherwise silent, tense room.

Obviously there had been a racial dispute, and in our tank, the race I belong to was outnumbered eleven to two. If I had been there, it would have been eleven to three. I felt sick. Both injured inmates were hospitalized with serious injuries. With my heart in my throat, I breathed a silent prayer to Jesus, my Protector, Savior, and only Friend inside these walls.

Go ahead, ask me how important it is to attend church. Ask me how I know I have a supernatural Father who has assigned at least one guardian angel, and in my case maybe more, to watch me 24/7. Had I not been in church, I would have been hospitalized too. Who told the deputy to open the gate? Why hadn't I been in that dayroom, fighting for my life? "The angel of the Lord encamps around those who fear him / and he delivers them" (Psalm 34:7).

How important is attending church? Sometimes more important than you'll ever know.

Jesus was preparing me for my future. By giving me tangible, undeniable miracles, He strengthened my feeble faith. Yet often I'd still wonder, *Where are You, God?* and just about that time He'd lay another one on me.

One Tuesday morning breakfast had been served, and the deputy called for clothing exchange. Twice a week we got clean laundry issued. Tuesday—jumpsuits, towels, boxers, socks, and shirts. Fridays—sheets, boxers, socks, and shirts. I never changed my jumpsuit—everything else, but not my jumpsuit. It is hard to get decent clothing, especially jumpsuits, so when I finally finessed a nice one, I kept it! It had taken a few months of trading, begging, and buying to find it, and I planned to keep it. I washed it, pressed it, mended it, and creased it—keeping it looking nice for those all too-short visits on Saturdays and Sundays.

I pulled on my suit, grabbed my laundry, and joined the inmates walking down the hallway to the room where we exchanged our dirty clothes. This morning I noticed a new deputy standing off to the side as we marched, single file, down the hall.

We lined up and began exchanging. As I reached the table, the new deputy sauntered toward me. I kept looking forward, trying not to attract his attention.

Just then a deep voice said, "Jumpsuit change." My heart skipped a beat. He couldn't be talking to me! Then he thumped my shoulder and yelled, "I said, 'jumpsuit change'!" I felt a wave of hate flash through me as I started a feeble excuse as to why I didn't want to change my suit. But I failed miserably and began to unsnap my favorite suit. I could only imagine what was in store for me as the clothing attendant handed me a clean jumpsuit. Seeing the deputy smiling smugly made my blood boil. To him it was a game. He watched my helpless anger, hoping I would retaliate to give him a reason to use physical force. I knew that, no matter what, the deputies would win any type of confrontation. My only choice was to cooperate.

I took the suit and headed back to my cell. I didn't even want to look at it because I knew it would be a total "wino" issue. I hoped it wouldn't be too tight. In jail, tight-fitting suits cause trouble. I had seen many fights over things like this, and I didn't want to be the center of attention.

I felt so angry I saw red. *Those awful guards!* I reached my cell, unrolled the suit, and held it at arm's length. What a sight! Worse than I'd ever seen or even imagined. But with no choice, I put it on. Yes, it was the tight, form-fitting suit I had dreaded. I was devastated. I couldn't understand why God would allow this to happen to me. Had I been too proud of my neatly pressed, creased suit? Was I so vain that God needed to teach me a lesson?

Right then and there I prayed, earnestly asking God for a suit that fit. Nothing special, just a decent fit. Afterward I felt silly. In the grand scheme of things, it seemed a rather petty thing to pray about.

About an hour later when we were allowed to go to the dayroom, another inmate approached me, eyeing my suit. I waited for the teasing I knew would start. But to my surprise he said, "Skip, my suit's too big. Would you trade?"

Wow! Who was I to argue about a bigger suit? Especially one way better than the first.

A few minutes later another inmate asked to trade because his suit was too baggy. The second suit fit better yet! *God worked fast,* I thought. I had been in the dayroom only ten minutes, and here I had a jumpsuit that fit.

The next day I began to look more and more at my pitiful jumpsuit. As I stared at it draped over the bars, I started to pray. *God, would it be too much to ask You for my old jumpsuit back?* Maybe it was pride, but I missed having a nice suit.

On Friday afternoon God gave me the final answer to my prayer. As I sat in my cell reading, my bunkie called to me from the dayroom. "Hey, Skip. What would you pay to have your old jumpsuit back?" I thought he was teasing. He knew how much I missed my suit.

"Come on, don't joke about that anymore," I protested.

"Seriously, Skip. Come and look."

He pointed to an inmate who had arrived earlier that day. My mouth dropped open as my gaze settled on my old jumpsuit with its pressed cuffs and handmade creases.

An hour later, with a bag of popcorn and a few chocolate bars as payment, I had successfully retrieved my lost suit. I sat in my cell and looked it over. It had some new wrinkles, meaning it had been machine washed and dried.

There were 3,500 inmates in this facility. My jumpsuit had traveled through the laundry service with thousands of others. If it came back to me by chance, I calculated it to be about .00028 percent. If you don't believe in prayer, your chances are no better than buying a lotto ticket!

The most important thing is not the fact that I now sported my old jumpsuit. It was the comfort in knowing that God, my God, the One who parted the Red Sea and closed the hungry lions' mouths and created you and me, still takes time to hear the smallest, most insignificant prayers. Even one about a jumpsuit! We can ask Him for anything in His name and He will do it (see John 14:14).

One day I felt like talking to a guy in jail who had allegedly killed a twenty-month-old child. The coroner's report stated he did not abuse the baby, but his crime is still not acceptable among convicts. I didn't think they'd take him out; but they probably would severely beat him wherever he went within the prison system. I walked by his cell and found him reading Genesis and doing a Bible study. I'd never spoken to him before, so he acted a bit surprised. I asked him if he had read the New Testament, and he replied "Yes, a few times." Then he grabbed a book from his desk and asked if I'd ever read it. It was *Steps to Christ*! I smiled Yes, and he said he just couldn't believe how inspired this woman was. He'd never read a book that kept hitting him over and over the way this one did. He liked it as much as some of Paul's writings. Wow! Then I told him she was a Seventh-day Adventist writer and grabbed some tracts and a couple of Christian books from my cell for him. He told me he'd had trouble getting Christian literature, so I opened the "Adventist Book Center store" in my cell and flooded his cell with good stuff. I felt bad for not sharing sooner. That old snake kept the barrier high, but I thanked God for the strength He gave me that day. Unfortunately, I'm pretty sure I'm the only one who had ever spoken to him.

Chapter 23

TRUE
CHRISTIANITY

Peaple outside imagine incarceration as a boring and color-less existence. For many inmates it is, but not for me. From the moment I arrived at OCJ, I was filled with the Spirit. God was active in every facet of my life. The complexity of God's plan often caused me to sit and marvel as I again and again noticed His perfect timing. Many individuals wrote to me—some I'd known as a child, some I'd never met. But all had one common theme: Christ and His love. Letters told of prayer circles on my behalf all over the country. I cherished mention of prayer support and spent time thanking every person in letters and thanking God in prayer. I felt overwhelmed by the feeling of adoption and love from a church and faith I had spat on. This love is true Christianity, and I wanted to be part of it.

Myrna Tetz, a friend of my family since my parents' college days, organized one prayer circle on my behalf, and I received three letters besides hers from people who attended these prayer sessions. In the previous ten to twelve years, I had worked in a field in which I received mail only when someone wanted something. So I rejoiced when letters came from people who didn't want anything except for me to love the Lord with all my heart!

This love seemed hard for me to grasp and even harder for me to believe all that was happening, like an impossible dream coming true. I felt accepted into a very large, loving family that stretched from coast to coast. I wanted to do something with, for, and in the church when I paroled, although I didn't know what because I had trained only for pitching and sales, but I wanted to share my story and my conversion with people young and old.

Myrna also determined to find a suitable person in the area who would visit me. She phoned the union, the conference, and the college offices, getting assurances that someone would visit.

Three weeks later no one had visited me yet. She repeated her phone calls; again people promised to visit, but again no one came. One morning as she complained to the Lord that He hadn't impressed *anyone* to visit, a name came to her mind—Cyril Connelly—a man she thought unsuitable for a visit as he wasn't a minister, and she doubted we would have anything in common.

But she followed up on the impression and phoned. An assistant answered saying Cyril wasn't in, she didn't know when he would return, and she didn't know where to reach him. So Myrna hung up the phone and went on with her work.

The next morning someone knocked on Myrna's office door. Cyril Connelly stood in the doorway. Dumbfounded, she greeted him warmly and asked him to sit down because she had something to tell him.

After she had, as she said, "babbled on and on" with the story of my parents' request, the phone calls, the disappointments, and his name coming to her mind as an answer to prayer, Cyril responded ever so quietly, "Myrna, I'll go."

And go he did. Early one morning, I heard my name blasted over the loudspeaker while I lay a million miles away in dreamland. "Fleck, get up and get ready. You've got a visit." Completely unprepared, I hurriedly groomed. When the cell door creaked open, I walked down the long tier still tying my shoes and straightening my collar. *Who would be coming to see me?* I wondered to myself. I didn't know anyone in the area, didn't expect anyone, so who could it be?

In the visiting room, I scanned the many faces on my way to the assigned booth and then looked through the glass at an unfamiliar face. Double-checking my booth number, I slowly sat down and picked up the phone receiver. A gray-haired gentleman picked up the opposite receiver and with a warm and hearty smile said, "Hello, Rick. My name's Cyril Connelly, and I am a friend of Myrna Tetz. She said we should meet."

Still trying to put it all together, I smiled and thanked him for coming. We had a nice forty-five-minute visit ending with Cyril telling me he'd see me again soon.

And see me again he did! Again and again for three-and-a-half years his sometimes sleepy but always smiling face would keep me entertained and uplifted. Cyril had lived in Oshawa, Ontario, and both of us were Canadians, so we knew some of the same people. We had similar, often-used humor systems. Every week Cyril got up very early on Friday (a visiting day), went to his office to get the day's work done, and then drove to the jail, a half hour away. He'd have to wait for an hour or more before he could see me. Then he'd sit on a stool in front of a glass window with me on the other side and use a telephone for our forty-five-minute visit. Later, Cyril managed to get ministerial credentials and could visit any day he wished.

Cyril was one of the first to demonstrate true Christianity to me. He expected nothing in return for his time and sacrifice, and I marveled at his commitment, and still do, as he and his entire family have become like my second family, constantly supporting and loving this often lonely convict.

Now that I'm in another area several hundred miles away, weekly letters and occasional visits have kept our friendship alive. Cyril's willingness to minister to me and my family as Christ would have ministered has blessed many.

One day while waiting to be ushered into our little chapel, I caught a glimpse of a face I'd not seen for some time. Instantly my pulse quickened, and I wanted to run—not an option. Slowly we moved forward until the door closed when all were seated. The service became a blur as I focused all my attention to my right; two pews ahead sat Clavo. A thousand sights, sounds, and images flashed through my mind: cold, death, fear, anger. *Did he come to kill me? Will he tell his homeboys in my tank to do it?* The devil tried to suffocate me with fear.

Silently I began to pray for protection. Then, as if splashed by cool water, clarity came—he's in church! *Can it be? Does he know Jesus?* I couldn't believe that. After all, I knew him well. But why then did he sing with the rest and appear to pray? I studied his every move as he participated in the service.

A day later a Hispanic guy I knew pulled me to the side and asked quietly, "Do you know Clavo?" Panic-stricken, I said to myself, *This is it—when I say Yes, he's going to run a knife into my heart.* Staring without expression, he waited. I looked around, trying to accept what was about to happen, and finally replied, "Yes." Quickly his hand disappeared into his pocket—I gasped, sure of what would follow—only to watch him produce a folded paper with my name printed on it. "Clavo told me to give this to you," he said and disappeared.

Shaking legs guided me back to my bunk, where I tore off the tape and began to read. "Rick. Respects to you and praise God for His grace. . . ." When I finished reading, tears spilled down my cheeks. Clavo had given his life to Christ! For the next three and a half years, whenever we saw each other at church and court appearances, Clavo always had his pocket Bible with him.

With only three of us in custody, my defense lawyer didn't hold high hopes. The district attorney had a double homicide to solve, and he was convinced three men had entered the trailer. We tried to get my case separated from the other two but failed.

I felt down for a day or so when the ruling on the motion to separate my trial from the other two was denied, but thanks to the peace that passes understanding, I was spared the agony of serious depression. I became more upset about my faith being so shallow than about the actual ruling. Of course, I didn't recognize it until a day or two later. Then I had to get on my knees and repent for being such a weakling. Although legally it was a minor setback, spiritually, it was a stroke of genius on God's part. Since I'd been busted, I'd never had a real test of my faith. I'd had most of my prayers answered, but because of the continual postponements, my faith in God's legal prowess had not been exercised. Now the time had come to really put things in His hands. I had a long way to go to reach that mustard seed!

As my brother said, "Why would God provide an easy solution to Rick's problem? Rick's never taken the easy road; why start now?" That was a valid point. I needed to get the most education from this situation in order to increase my faith, but I felt especially sad for my mom's and dad's sakes—my life has already caused them too much pain. For them, I wished the trial were over.

I had a friend on death row in San Quentin who wrote me because I'd sent him an *Adventist Review* article about death row with an address for others in the same situation. He asked where to get the *Review*. I thought to myself, *Hello, Holy Spirit, what a way to get to condemned men!* I asked Myrna Tetz to send him a subscription. We prisoners tend to be like pack rats—we hate to throw anything away, especially magazines. I knew they would circulate through the cells and the hearts of California's walking dead.

After many twists and turns, the trial date was set. Clavo, my other codefendant, and I would be tried together. The fourth had never been identified or arrested. The next two months would be the most traumatic of my life. With tons of evidence stacked squarely between me and freedom, the trial began. Each night I'd read a psalm, meditate on it, and write a message of encouragement to my parents, who faithfully sat right behind me every day. Often I heard a sob or sigh. I wasn't going through this alone—they were devastated too.

Every day I watched the victims' families on the other side of the courtroom who stared at me, perhaps trying to imagine what kind of monster would do what I was accused of. Unable to speak, I'd sit silently praying for hours and trying not to cry as the forensic evidence was displayed in full detail, making me sick to my stomach. Having no one to talk to, I'd write, pouring out my heart and hope in Christ.

December 24, 1997
Dear Friends in Christ,

I'm halfway through my trial—not an easy time but the Lord is working miracles. My father and mother as well as the Connellys and a few others are with me, and my Christian family has kept me inundated with letters of faith, hope, and love.

My eyes are focused on Jesus, our Redeemer and Savior, who has already given me far more than I deserve. I beg you to each cling to His promises and pray without ceasing.

Second Corinthians 5:7 tells us to live by faith, not by sight. When things look grim and you don't see God, be assured He is there. He'll never leave you nor forsake you. I encourage you to keep spreading the Word.

Your prayers for me are appreciated far more than you'll ever know. My prayer is that we will all be together in heaven, if not before.

Thanks for your support. God bless you. Never lose focus on the center of your life—Jesus Christ.
Your brother in Christ,
Rick

Chapter 24

THE
VERDICT

At Christmas, we were given a break from the proceedings, a welcome pause in a grueling ordeal. Once the holidays were over, the trial resumed. One morning the judge announced an unexpected recess. Our lawyers looked agitated, and the district attorney appeared angry as they filed into the judge's chambers. A short time later, while the three of us waited in a side holding cell, Clavo's lawyer appeared. He and Clavo talked briefly in hushed tones; then just as quickly, the lawyer disappeared.

Clavo came over and sat between me and my codefendant. "OK, Guys," he began quietly. "You and I know what really happened that night. I am guilty," he barely whispered. "But the DA has offered me a deal of twenty years with half the time; that means I'll be out in ten." His words stung as they registered. "I told my lawyer I'd discuss it with you guys and then give my answer. I won't take the deal if you don't OK it." We stared at each other silently. I stood and faced the blank wall. *Why not me, Lord?* I silently asked my Savior. But no answer came. After a couple minutes of silence, I nodded and said, "Praise God, Clavo, He's delivered you. Praise God."

His lawyer returned, guards removed him from the holding cell, and I never saw Clavo again. Just the two of us remained at the defendant's table, and from that point on, it became clear that justice would not be served in this case. Seven days later both of us stood as the verdict was about to be read.

The courtroom was hushed; the jurors sat uncomfortably, probably glad jury duty was over, some no doubt wondering if they had made the right decision. The jury foreman handed the verdict to the judge who, after lowering his glasses and reading briefly, passed it to the clerk. My knees weakened, and every part of my body shook.

"In the case of the State of California versus Rick Fleck . . ."

Oh God, please don't let it be guilty. Please, Lord, please, I begged silently as I stood terrified.

"We the jury find the defendant . . ." I stopped breathing. "Guilty."

"Guilty." The sound of the clerk's voice pierced the silence as she read the verdict. Like a giant balloon, the tension burst in the courtroom. The prosecution's side clapped; my side cried. In my shock, everything seemed to move in slow motion, and I couldn't make out the words spoken by the clerk or the judge. Everything seemed surreal. Like driving in a fog, I couldn't find a reference point. Many things have affected my life, but nothing bigger than that one word: *guilty.*

As guards took me back to my cell, time began to tick by again. I felt sick to my stomach, light-headed, and weak. The walls were closing in, and my mind began to spin. *This can't be. I didn't do it. I didn't do it.*

I had given my life to the Lord five years prior to this conviction. How could He have let me be convicted of a crime I didn't commit? I lay on my mattress, alone in my cell, half crying, half cursing everyone and everything. A few hours passed, and finally, late in the evening, I fell asleep. I'd heard that depression causes people to sleep, and it's the truth. The next day came and went. My parents had left for the week because they were allowed to visit only on the weekends. I got up to eat and went right back to sleep.

I woke the following day feeling such sorrow; yet from somewhere sprang a spark of joy. I then got on my knees and reintroduced myself to God, laying everything out, detail by detail. *God,* I prayed, *I thought I was supposed to win my case, marry a Christian girl, and preach the gospel to the world. I thought You were going to make me a mighty warrior for You. I thought You were beside me all the way. Was I wrong?*

Eventually I realized I had a self-centered, self-constructed understanding of God. The small spark of joy grew, and I knew that at some point, God would reveal Himself to me in a new and awesome way.

Prior to the verdict, I had witnessed for several years. God had allowed me to be a part of some wonderful answers to prayer. I had seen men walk out of jail. I had seen men give their lives to Christ. I'd seen hardened convicts melt in the presence of the Holy Spirit. I figured I would walk out of jail and serve God, giving testimony to all that He'd let me see and do. While I was on my knees, God revealed my devastating misconception.

All those future plans were products of my imagination and my wishes; I had misled myself. God's plans hadn't changed a bit. From the time I gave my life to Him in December 1993 until the day of my conviction in January 1998, God's plan for me had not wavered. I never had really given Him complete control and let Him do with me what He wanted. Sure, I had prayed for guidance and direction, but as most people when given directions, I'd find some way to do things my own way and often get lost in the process.

A "not guilty" verdict would have meant that all my plans were a go. The word *guilty* meant that I had no agenda. I had made all my plans and based them on *my* ideas of what God was going to do for *me.* I had not remembered that by giving my life to Him, I had given Him control. The important next step was not what God would do for me—He'd done enough already. The question now became, What would I do for Him?

When I rose from my knees, the spark of joy began to burn; I was excited. A new life was on its way, and I knew God was in control.

Later that day I wrote a short note to all who had supported me through prayer and mail.

January 1998
Dear Brothers and Sisters in Christ,

I cried, I wallowed in self-pity, and I sat and wondered. After a few confusing days, I reached out to the hand that never left me. Praise God, His grace is sufficient for me.

The many prayers offered on my behalf did not fall on deaf ears. God's clock is not Swiss, and I'm thankful for that. How can I expect Him to start marching to my band? He waited twenty-plus years to answer my parents' prayers for my salvation. The important thing is that their prayers were answered. In that same way, by that same God, your prayers for me will be answered too.

My fear now is that some of you may lose heart after the apparent refusal by God to grant your requests. Please don't stop trusting in faith, hope, and love; hurt and sorrow can cloud the bluest of skies. Just remember that beyond those clouds lives not the temporal master of this earth, but the eternal God of the universe. No human judge has ever had the final say for any of God's children. I may not have my physical freedom today, but I am free on the inside. What else matters?

Now our communication will have to continue through letters and occasional phone calls. God is good, and His love endures forever. He has not forsaken me nor forgotten me. He's right here with me today. I thank you for your prayers. Thank you for the many ways you have supported me in the past. Take heart. It's not over yet.
Your brother in Christ,
Rick Fleck aka Skip

Chapter 25

MIRACLE
LAWYER

Guilty—the word took on a life of its own and filled my mind both awake and asleep. Fortunately, due to some technicalities, the DA decided not to seek the death penalty; instead, he sought a sentence of life without the possibility of parole. LWOP, an acronym for my sentence, means I will die in prison.

With the verdict final, I was left with a choice that many in my situation must make. Should I throw away my Bible and faith and with it any hope of one day seeing my Lord and Savior? Or should I get real with God and learn *His* will for me? The choice was obvious, and it didn't take long for me to fall to my knees apologizing for my faithlessness and asking for a new attitude and defined direction.

God answered obviously and quickly. The first request I put before the throne in supplication was a test of sorts to determine God's hand in my new life as a convicted murderer. (The term *convicted murderer* still haunts me today, and I refuse to wear the label.) Immediately after hearing the verdict, my parents and I decided an appeal had to be filed.

The process is long and tedious with usually disappointing results. According to statistics, 78 percent of all appeals are reaffirmed guilty, 19 percent are modified, resulting in a change in sentencing, and only 3 percent are overturned, resulting in freedom. It takes a miracle to be in the 3 percent, but the God I serve is in the miracle business. The state supplies convicts with bare minimum appeal assistance that inevitably ends with a denial and all hope of reversal lost. We decided to ask God to reveal *His* plan for my life in a unique way.

I previously had read George Mueller's autobiography, a magnificent story of faith and answered prayer. Using Mueller's method of telling no one except God of our wants and needs, we began praying daily. Our prayers were specific. *Lord, if the results of the trial and verdict are part of Your plan and I'm to spend the rest of my life in prison, then deny this request. I ask only that You give me the strength to accept Your decision. But, Lord, if it is Your will that someday I walk out a free man, then grant our request and supply a lawyer paid in full. Thank You, gracious Savior.* Our prayers filled the heavens. The answer to His will would be either Yes, in which case an adequate lawyer would be found and paid in full, or No, which would mean that although I'd been convicted wrongly, I would spend the rest of my life in prison.

Either answer would be accepted, and we would praise our Lord. My parents spent the next week searching for the lawyer God would provide. After interviewing attorneys and praying over their names, they chose Bill Kopeny. His résumé spoke for itself. But a major hurdle amounted to twenty-five thousand dollars plus another ten thousand dollars for the additional writ of habeas corpus to follow *if* the direct appeal failed. My jaw dropped when my parents told me the price. Twenty-five thousand might as well have been twenty-five million to a penniless person like me.

OK, God, let's see what You want to do, I prayed. We told the lawyer we'd get back to him as soon as funds became available. Each day I brought the sum to God and asked Him for His answer. Within a few days my parents got a call from a group of their friends whom I'd never met. One gentleman tactfully explained that the group had put together a sum of money just in case it was needed for my defense. He didn't know if, in fact, any was needed but explained they had put nine thousand dollars in an account in my father's name. With tears of gratitude and joy, my father thanked him, promising to let him know if we needed the funds. Nine thousand dollars—beautiful—and we thanked God profusely. But we also knew that without the balance, God's answer was No, and I'd spend my life in prison, which I would accept as God's will.

For the next few days, I spoke to my parents by phone, and we prayed without ceasing. Then came an amazing call from a distant relative. Unaware of our plight, this woman contacted Mom and Dad. First she offered her sympathy in my recent conviction, and then she told them she'd received sixteen thousand dollars in an income tax refund and, if needed, the money would be theirs as a gift. With tears rolling down my face, I listened to the incredible story over the phone. We needed twenty-five thousand, and twenty-five thousand was provided—no more and no less. Does Jesus answer prayer? Oh, yes, and He's exact. With my appellate lawyer secured, I thanked God over and over for His obvious, unmistakable answer to prayer. With God's answer to my request so spectacular, I decided to serve Him boldly. I set out to be a fisher of men and prayed each morning for the ability to recognize even the smallest windows of opportunity in which to witness for Him.

A second equally incredible miracle involving my appellate attorney occurred later, a miracle that would test the limits of my faith. But the task at hand was to sow seeds and serve God, and each day brought new, exciting challenges.

Soon I once again sat on a bus bound for prison. But this situation was different in many ways. Now a "lifer," I felt no giddy feelings of knowing I'd be out soon. I didn't know the future. I'd be housed in a maximum-security prison, the likes of which I'd only heard about. Rumors swirled of killings, riots, and mindless daily violence. Men with nothing to lose and much to prove roamed the yards in packs like sharks looking for opportunities to attack. I was frightened.

I watched as my breath fogged the cool windows of the bus. I watched the beautiful green hills roll by and wondered if I'd ever see one again. A cow, a horse, and a quaint farmhouse—I stared intently trying to burn the passing images into my mind hoping someday to trade them for the oppressive sight of four cell walls. *Oh, Lord, my strength and my God. I need You today and every day. I am so alone.* This and many other prayers left my lips and mind often. God never stayed away, and His angels always held me close.

Once again I entered the reception-center prison, waiting for my classification and subsequent transfer to what would be my new home. God didn't waste any of the time I had promised to Him. He assigned my first discipleship mission soon after I had settled into my prison cell.

As Jesse stood in the dayroom with his life's belongings over his shoulder, I looked out my cell door wondering who'd be the unlucky one to be stuck with him. The next thing I knew, my cell door opened, the corrections officer said, "Cell 116," and pointed Jesse my way.

I was stunned. My first celly had just left, and it usually takes a few days for another to move in. Second, I had prayed to God for an older, low-key person for my celly.

As Jesse walked into the cell, I could tell just by his looks that he wasn't going to be what I'd planned.

During July in Southern California, the cells are unusually hot. Once inside, Jesse immediately took off his jumpsuit and shirt and confirmed my worst nightmares—he was a head-to-toe White supremacist. Neo-Nazi tattoos covered his body. He had all the markings and evidently had earned his stripes on the battlefields of the prison system. As I gazed at his various decorations, I silently prayed for strength to endure what I thought would be in store for me.

Jesse tossed his bag on the bunk, and before I could say anything, he began pouring out his heart. He told me that he'd just been in a fight in another building, and the guy he beat up was telling on him. This meant his good time would be taken away, and he'd serve three more months. Then, in the next breath, he explained that his wife had been sending him a letter a day but had abruptly stopped writing.

As I listened, I wondered how God could be so cruel to me. I forgot my recent decision to be a witness. All I could think about was my disappointment that God hadn't given me a celly of my choosing.

The night before I had asked God to lead me in His paths and make me a witness to others. Now here a young man stood in front of me crying out for help, and I could think only of myself. Obviously memory wasn't my strong point.

Jesse finally just had snapped and had taken out his anger on the weakest person he could find in the other building. That's why guards moved him to my building. As he went through his story, Jesse pulled out pictures and, with tears in his eyes, told me his life wasn't worth living without his wife.

In prison men do not openly display tears. Most men would be lying if they said they hadn't cried, but they rarely cry in front of another inmate. I didn't know what to do. I silently prayed for help, but nothing came to mind.

Slowly Jesse calmed down and soon just sat on his bunk with head hanging low. I changed the subject and breathed a sigh of relief. We talked until we fell asleep.

We'd no sooner awakened the next morning, a Friday, and Jesse started stressing again. When it came time for my devotional, I took out my Bible and opened it. As soon as I started to read, Jesse became very quiet.

About five minutes later, he said, "I tried that Bible stuff. It didn't work."

I stopped reading. "When?" I asked.

"About a week ago," he replied.

"What happened?"

"I asked God to give me a letter from my wife, and when it didn't come, I took my Bible and threw it across the dayroom."

At that point I thought this guy might be way beyond any help I could possibly give him. And I was right. I couldn't help him, but God had other plans.

"Who gave up first?" I asked Jesse after a moment. "You or God?"

"I did," he answered.

Then I asked, "What would it take for you to believe in Christ and to let Him into your life?"

He smiled sarcastically and laid out his deal: "I want a letter from my wife saying she loves me and will wait for me, and I want my wife to have enough money to live on as long as I'm in prison."

"OK," I said. "Then that's what we're going to ask for. If God takes care of your wife and you get a letter from her, would you give your life to Him?"

"Yes," Jesse said.

I was amazed.

Jesse had begun his life of crime at the age of nine by trying to set his school bus on fire and getting himself sent to a boys' home. By thirteen he was convicted of car theft and sent to the California Youth Authority. There, he joined a gang and adopted White supremacist ideals. Due to many violent offenses while in the California Youth Authority, he never did parole as planned. He stayed there until the age of eighteen and then, deemed too violent for parole, was sent to prison and not paroled until the age of twenty-one. When he was out of prison, he married and began a family, only to violate parole nine months later and re- ceive another six months. This is when I met him.

Here was a hardened White supremacist gang member will- ing to give all up, if God would answer his requests. I have to be honest, I had doubts. Not only did I doubt that God would fully answer our prayers, but I also doubted that Jesse would believe in Jesus if God did answer his prayer as we requested.

At 10:00 A.M. Saturday morning—the very next day—the floor officer knocked at the door, holding a letter in his hand. He called Jesse's last name. I couldn't believe it, and Jesse was in shock. Before he opened the letter, I said, "Is that fast enough for you?"

Jesse smiled, put down the letter, and asked if we could pray. Still stunned, I knelt with him and simply thanked God for sending him a letter. He opened the letter and began reading it aloud. His wife apologized for not writing and explained that she'd run out of money. She told him her parents had asked her to move home and stay as long as she needed to and that all their needs were being met. Then she told him how much she loved him and that she would be at the gate to pick him up when he paroled. She ended the letter with hugs and kisses.

I don't think I've ever seen a face glow as brightly as Jesse's did. The anger was gone. The fear had left, and there was a look of peace in his eyes.

From that point on, Jesse was a different person. He began reading his Bible—and not just to pass the time. For hours on end, he'd read and ask questions. We read together and did Bible studies daily. Jesse's relationship with Jesus grew so fast it blew me away. Many times I awoke in the middle of the night to find him praying or reading the Bible.

A couple weeks later a package from my parents arrived containing a book called *Jack*. Immediately Jesse asked to read it, and as he began to read the book, a whole new set of questions arose.

"What's a Seventh-day Adventist?" he asked.

Oh boy, I thought. *Now what am I going to do? I'm not versed enough to go into the dos and don'ts and whys of the Adventist religion. I know my beliefs but not how to put them across without causing unanswerable questions.* I prayed that God would help me find the words to tell him about Adventists.

A day later I noticed Jesse still deep in the book. As a matter of fact, he read the book cover to cover, stopping only to sleep. When he finished, he asked if I thought Bakersfield, California, had an Adventist church.

God had answered yet another prayer. He'd given me that book to tell Jesse about Seventh-day Adventists.

Soon Jesse began to tell me about his dreams of what he wanted to do when he got out. He began with being baptized and ended with speaking to young adults about the power of Jesus Christ. Gone was the racial prejudice, the lumberjack vocabulary subsided, and Jesse gradually became a man of God. He began telling others in the building about his incredible answer to prayer.

But it didn't end there. Jesse still had to go to a formal hearing with the lieutenant for a decision on how much extra time he would receive for fighting. Jesse knew he was guilty, and he also realized that as a Christian, he couldn't lie about what happened that day. Jesse struggled with the decision for days. Without witnesses, it would be his word against the victim's. If found guilty, he would receive three extra months. If not, he'd go home in a few weeks.

The day finally came for Jesse's hearing, and as he left the building, I sent up a silent prayer, asking God to make the lieutenant notice the change in Jesse and the remorse he had for hitting the weaker inmate.

Thirty minutes later Jesse returned, and by the glow on his face, I knew something good had happened. He'd walked into the lieutenant's office and sat down. The lieutenant asked to see his knuckles. Then he said, "In the interest of justice, I'm going to find you not guilty. You may go."

The Lord had taken this man and in a matter of weeks changed him and his life forever.

I was transferred shortly after, but I'll never forget the tears shed the night I left. Jesse's experience changed more than Jesse. The Lord showed me He could work anywhere and anytime, and He could change anyone.

BEGINNING A
LIFE SENTENCE

Susanville, a northern California town nestled in a beautiful valley, lies in the shadow of Thompson Peak. This quaint town, filled with California mining history, now serves the state by accommodating two full-size prisons. The oldest is CCC, California Correctional Center or "Susy's House" for short. The newer, a maximum-security prison, is called High Desert State Prison. These two prisons house more than eight thousand convicted felons.

The bus veered sharply as it turned into the entrance of my new home, High Desert State Prison. After two months in reception and several close encounters with God, I would now serve at base camp for whatever mountains He had prepared for me to climb. I heard scuttlebutt at reception such as, "You don't want to go to High Desert, but if you end up there, be prepared for the worst." Rumors of ongoing violence, including a recent riot resulting in the death of an inmate, sent shivers through my body as we shuffled off the bus and into the holding cells. Immediately guards separated us by race, obviously implying ongoing racial tension throughout the prison.

High Desert has four primary yards labeled A through D; C and D yards, designed for the worst criminals, house mostly men who thrive on plotting and carrying out violence. Due to my crime and affiliation with gang members, the classification committee deemed me a potential threat and assigned me to C yard for a minimum of three years. My mouth dropped open and my stomach lurched as I listened to the lieutenant delivering the ugly news. "Fleck, you're a straight-up 180 [a number assigned to the violent housing units] and will be for at least three years—dismissed!"

With that, I shuffled back to the holding cell, trying to understand how this could be possible. *Why, Lord, would You put me on a yard known statewide for being one of the most violent? Lord, please make this be a mistake.* Silence. Only the sound of chains and of inmates murmuring and rummaging through sack lunches filled the air. I felt scared and alone, abandoned and defeated. The fragile faith of a new Christian must cause God to hold His breath as a father would watching his son swim in the deep end of a pool for the first time. But God in His omniscience allowed me to struggle, fail, and swallow water often before reaching down and pulling me to safety. His lifelines always came in the form of answered prayers.

A few hours later I found myself and a couple of others with our state issue bundle of clothing and bedding walking across the desolate grassless war zone called "the yard." We moved single file, struggling to hold everything while handcuffed tightly. Guards escorted us to our housing units and showed us to our cells. An overwhelming smell of stale cigarette smoke, body odor, and alcohol filled my nostrils as I stepped inside.

Because the cell was dimly lit, I fumbled for the light switch, and after turning it on, wished I'd left it off. The walls were covered to the ceiling with explicit pornography taken from magazines. Seated on the bunk cross-legged sat an ashen-complexioned man smoking a cigarette and smiling a toothless grin. "Hi, there, Homeboy. I'm Corky," he said and stuck out his hand for a shake. Mustering a smile, I unloaded my bundle and shook his hand. "I'm Skip. Nice to meet you." I strained a nod and sat down heavily.

Nervous but exhausted, I sat and listened as my new celly explained the program to me. "OK, check it out Holmes . . . ," he began using every foul and derogatory racial slur and swear word available. "We're at war with the Blacks. It's our turn to blast them at the first unlock. Stuff's been going on back and forth for sixteen months now, and it's our turn, so if you get a chance, it's a green light on Blacks. If you don't take the opportunity, you'll be dealt with." His prison jargon droned on as my tired body begged for sleep after an anxiety-filled day. I wanted only to close my eyes and fade off into a land that normally would give me relief—sleep—the only true escape.

Corky was filled with hate and anger and bent on letting me know the expectations of a White convict. When he finished, I asked where I should put my stuff. Pointing to the top locker and bunk, he flopped back on his bed, giving me room to get organized. Having no personal property and desperately needing to read some scriptures, I asked if he had a Bible. To my surprise, he did. "Thank you," I said and reclined on my bunk between the porno-covered walls. Praying and reading gave me instant relief as God filled my space, and I immediately felt safe. Not wanting to think about the next day, I said, "Good night" and soon slipped into a place I enjoyed.

*   *   *   *   *

The C yard is divided into two facilities, upper and lower. The upper yard had been on lockdown (L/D—meaning inmates leave their cells only three times a week for showers) for sixteen months due to the rioting, but it was scheduled to come off L/D for a trial run in a couple of months. Fearing I'd be caught in the violence, I prayed daily for deliverance from a dire situation.

The next few weeks were terrible. Corky had a batch of home-made wine* brewing, which he tried repeatedly to get me to drink with him. I respectfully declined while watching him slobber, burp, and vomit, missing the toilet by a foot. The smell was putrid. I lay on my bunk listening to the night sounds wondering why God would allow me to live in such a foul place.

Next Corky scored some heroin and a dirty old needle, so for a few more days he mumbled and laughed—and vomited. Again I cried out to God begging for a cell change or anything that would make the situation better. Silence. Not a whisper did I hear. The weeks turned into months. Faithfully I read my Bible and spent quiet time with God while Corky slept.

After three months a guard came to my door, cuffed me up, and escorted me to the counselor's office. The counselor gave me some classification papers and inquired how I was doing. Sadly, I had to reply, "Fine." Then, oddly, the escorting officer asked if I was gang affiliated.

"No," I said quickly.

"Are you a programmer?"[†] he asked.

"Yes, absolutely," I answered.

"OK, let me see if I can find you a bed on the lower yard, which is not on lockdown. Would you like that?"

Barely believing what I heard, I responded, "Oh yes. Please, please, please." They both smiled. But soon I sat again in the dark, foul box called home, wondering when or if a move would happen.

I explained to Corky what had happened, and he wasn't too enthusiastic, knowing he could do a lot worse than me for a celly. He began trying to convince me to stay. I listened quietly but remained unconvinced. Then came one of the strangest conversations I've ever had. Corky asked if I wanted to hear a story. I said "Sure" and climbed down from my bunk to listen. He began, "Skip, I can see you are a Christian. Don't let anyone change you or say you can't be what God has made you. You may not believe me, but I, too, used to be sold-out for the Lord."

I couldn't believe what he said, but the tears welling up in his eyes left no question. He continued tearfully telling me how he had been deeply involved with a ministry for seven years. He'd married a Christian woman and been blessed with two wonderful daughters. The Lord reigned as the center of his life, and He had given him the desires of his heart.

But one day he weakened for a moment, Satan struck, and he fell. A simple, friendly drink at a bar began his complete meltdown. Seven years of blessings quickly vaporized, and within a couple of months, Corky found himself convicted and sentenced to life in prison. His choice to possess a controlled substance violated California's three-strikes law, so for possessing a couple of hundred dollars' worth of speed, he now will spend the rest of his life in prison. Watching him pour out his heart to me and, I believe, indirectly to Jesus, I felt instant compassion for this disheartened soul. He ended his story by asking for a book to read. Handing him Ellen White's *Steps to Christ*, I watched as he spent the next few days in quiet reading and praying, often reciting passages that reflected on Christ's love.

A few days later, the voice of the floor officer startled me. "Fleck, roll your stuff up. You're moving to the lower yard," he barked through the door. Excitement mixed with sadness gripped me as I quickly packed my meager belongings. Corky felt sad to see me go, and I, too, would miss his toothless smile, which I had seen often since his story that quiet night. God had thrown another lifeline once again, showing me only God truly knows the heart. He had a purpose when he stuck me in Corky's cell, and I couldn't leave until God's time was right.

Only a short walk brought me into what seemed like another world. Gone was the desolate dirt war zone void of life. Walking onto the lower yard made my heart sing. Handball players sweated in the sunshine, joggers moved around the track, and all kinds of activity melded into a mosaic of life. *This is program,* I thought to myself, *and I can't wait to get some fresh air.* Three and a half years in the county jail and another five months between reception and the locked-down upper yard made me more than eager to experience sunshine and fresh air. I inhaled deeply, enjoying the clean mountain breezes.

As the door closed behind me, I sat happily on the bunk of my new cell. "Thank You, Lord," I said aloud over and over. Whistling, I unpacked my things. I didn't care that the cell was filthy; it was home, and it was mine. "Thank You, Lord." Knowing no one, I wondered whom God would put in my path. Later that day a porter (inmate assigned to clean the housing unit) named Robert stopped by and introduced himself. Being the new guy and eager to learn about the program and who lived in our building, I enjoyed some small talk. Robert mentioned that his celly came from Orange County. "Oh, yeah? What's his name?" I asked. After being in the county jail fighting my case for three and a half years, I'd met a lot of guys on their way to prison.

"Dirk," he replied.

"Hey, I know a Dirk! Is he . . . ? I went on to describe the Dirk I knew.

"Yeah, that's him." Robert grinned. "Skip, did you know he's a Christian?"

"Really?" I mused out loud. "Well, tell him I'd like to say hello when he gets a chance to come by."

Robert nodded, said Goodbye, and continued down the tier pushing his broom. I remembered Dirk not as a Christian but as bloodied and bruised after being the second of two victims beaten senselessly in the dayroom during the riot I described earlier. Amazed, I praised God that he had not only recovered but also lived in the same building as a committed Christian brother, one of only a handful on this yard. I couldn't wait to catch up and listen to his conversion story. Since Dirk already had a younger celly whom he was teaching about Christ, I continued to pray that God would provide someone for me to teach also. Shortly God provided another building block of faith. I'll let Kenny tell about it in an article he wrote after we parted ways two and a half years later.

I know this is going to sound a bit crazy, but I'm glad I came to prison, because if I had not, I would not have found God. I was going down the road that leads to destruction, but the Lord delivered me, and the Lord should be all that matters in our lives. Whether I'm in here or out there, I will be doing the same thing—loving Jesus and telling others about Him. And in here, people need to know the Lord. This is sin city. Jesus says the healthy don't need the doctor, the sick do (Matthew 9:12).

Well, here's how I became a Christian and an Adventist:

I found myself in jail, charged with attempted murder. I was mad and afraid at the same time. Satan was in me—I could feel him. He was always there. I was mad all the time; in the morning or at night, it did not matter. I was sitting in my cell, mad like always. At what, I did not know. Then a cop appeared in front of the bars and said, "Get ready; you're going to court."

I got to court, and the judge told me my charges, among other things. As the cop walked me back to the cell, he asked how old I was. I told him eighteen. He then asked if I might be thinking of killing myself. I laughed at him, so he called the other cops. They took me to this room called the "rubber room." The floor was concrete with a hole in the ground for using the restroom. That was all that was in the room. They took all my clothes and put me in there. I remember how cold the floor felt.

I don't know how many days I was in there. I just remember a guy would come by, look at me, mark something on a paper, and then leave. Some time later a few cops opened the door, and one had a red jumpsuit in his hand. He told me to put it on, so I did. I asked where I was going, but the officer just looked at me and smiled.

They took me through a door, and there were people with cameras. Finally I saw the judge. *Why am I in court?*

I wondered. I found out the answer real fast. The judge said the person I shot was dead. I felt sick. I did not know what to do. The cops picked me up off the chair and rushed me out of the courtroom, right back to the rubber room. They ordered me to take off my clothes and then left me there.

I was having mixed feelings. I just kept saying, "This is not happening" over and over, until finally I just started crying and fell to my knees and told God, "I can't do this anymore. Help me and please come into my life and lead me. I don't want to live like this. I'm bad—help me to be good." I saw something in that rubber room that I can't explain, and I felt love like I have not felt before. I had to get my hands on a Bible. So, I got one and started reading. There were many things I did not understand. For example, verses about a beast coming out of the earth, a dragon chasing a lady, so I said, "Lord, lead me to someone who will show me."

I was sent to prison, and I saw Rick. We both were looking for a celly. I think Rick already had someone else in mind, and I did too. But the cop made a mistake and put me in the cell with Rick.

I still remember what Rick said when the door opened: "I thought you were someone else." I said to myself, "This is going to be a bad celly." Then I found out he was a Christian. And then he started telling me his beliefs, and I thought that everything he said about Adventists made sense, and the more I read, the more I became convinced that it was the remnant church.

I really believe God led me to Rick. In the beginning I thought Rick would be a bad celly, but not only did I find the best celly I have ever had, I found a brother in Christ. I pray that the Lord will lead others to people like Rick.

Kenny and I lived together for the next two and a half years studying and growing in the knowledge of the Lord. But not all was sunny and carefree. I soon found out that the smiles and apparent harmony on our yard were only a paper-thin facade masking the latent violence invisible only to the untrained eye of a fish like me. While playing handball one day shortly after arriving on the lower yard, I witnessed the first of many bloody scenes.

Eddy had a likeable air about him. An average Joe doing life and weighed down by the vices of prison, often drunk or high, Eddy always had a handshake for everyone. But Eddy had a secret. Prisons house racial hatred at its worst. All the lines are clearly drawn, and to step outside of them could cost an inmate his life. One weekend Eddy's girlfriend came to visit him. He'd told everyone she was bringing some drugs and soon the guys would be high. But he didn't mention that she was Black.

First thing Monday morning, after all the dope had been secretly passed out, three men attacked Eddy not more than ten feet from where I played handball. The attack was worse than anything I'd ever seen on TV. Taking him down, the three men repeatedly stabbed and sliced Eddy's face, head, and neck until only blood was recognizable, and the dirt around Eddy turned crimson. They were finished by the time the gunner in the tower realized what had happened and began to rain down gas and blocks from the block gun‡ strapped to his body. Shaking, I watched as the medics frantically tried to stop the bleeding. Eddy left on a stretcher, the assailants left in handcuffs, and almost immediately activities resumed as if nothing had happened. Eddy did survive, but I was shocked how such violence could erupt out of peace and then activity return to normal so quickly. I soon learned violence was the norm, and peace, the exception. I lost count of all the stabbings and after a while thought it strange if two weeks passed without violence.

Expecting a visit one weekend, I became increasingly upset when my door didn't open early Saturday morning. I spent the morning sulking and feeling abandoned, wondering what had happened. At 2:30 P.M. the unmistakable booming sounds of block guns filled the air. Loudspeakers blared as mayhem erupted just outside my building. Still stranded in my cell, I could only wonder what chaos ensued beyond. Before long we all saw the aftereffects of a full-scale racial riot. One by one guards escorted bloody and beat-up men back to their cells. The Mexicans had attacked the Whites, and many needed immediate hospital care.

Not until the following day, early Sunday morning when I finally sat with my day-late visitors, did I understand the extent of God's protection. Coming from Canada, my visitors were inexplicably delayed while customs officials examined and reexamined their citizenship papers, causing them to spend the night at the border. Had they not been delayed, I would have been exiting the visiting complex onto the yard at precisely 2:30 P.M., the exact time the riot broke out. I often wondered what would've happened had I been in the middle of that riot. Unbeknown to me, the question would be answered in years to come.

---

*Wine is made from crushed apples or any fruit, Kool-Aid®, and any form of sugar. It needs to sit for a four-to five-day period to ferment and turn into booze. Of course making and consuming wine is illegal.

†*Programmer* is prison lingo for someone who is willing to go with the program, adhere to the rules, and not cause trouble. A *knucklehead* is a nonprogrammer.

‡*Block gun* is the common name for a nonlethal weapon. It looks like a marine grenade launcher with a fat, short barrel that can shoot a variety of projectiles. A block round is a round that holds six tightly compressed rubber projectiles, approximately half an inch tall and half an inch around. They resemble a bottle cork, except they are rubber. They can take a person's wind or cause him to urinate blood if he's hit at close range. Guards shooting blocks are supposed to bounce them at inmates by trying to hit the ground first, but they don't always follow this regulation.

Chapter 27

THE

LIST

A lockdown always follows a riot. For most, lockdowns are tedious and trying because all inmates belonging to all races suffer. Locked down, commonly called "slammed," means exactly that. No program. Ten-minute showers three times a week is the extent of time out of the cell. We're handcuffed, escorted to a locking shower, then retrieved in the same fashion a short time later. Visits are conducted behind glass using a phone to communicate, and a strict one-hour time limit is often enforced.

I had to attack lockdowns in a different way. With nothing but time, I decided to use the days reading, studying, and writing. With each passing day, I began to see the face of God more and more clearly. Never before had I felt so close to Him. Kenny, my celly, also began making huge strides in his Christian walk. Lockdown became a time of meditating and pondering truths. Often the Holy Spirit would move me to write the ideas that were new to me.

I think the key to knowing God involves understanding the battle for our souls raging in unseen realms. In this battle there are no noncombatants; no one is exempt. And Satan's agents wear many different masks. In order to succeed in combat, we must put on the armor of God (see Ephesians 6:11–18), not just occasionally but daily. Prayer is the beginning of a relationship, the source of victory in such battles. Jesus offers, " 'Come to me, all you who are weary and burdened, and I will give you rest' " (Matthew 11:28). Too many times we emphasize correcting bad behavior before coming to God. The necessity of first quitting this or stopping that or giving up the other—that's a lie from Satan intended to discourage us. When discouraged, we are tempted to think, *I can't quit, so why try?* The truth is that we need to come to Christ first; His power will enable us to quit the bad behaviors. Nobody goes to a doctor after being healed. Now is the time to come to Jesus.

Every vice keeping one from Christ is a device of Satan. How can a person possibly beat an unseen force such as the devil? It's impossible without Christ, who is eager to form a relationship with all who want relief. How does such a relationship form? By prayer and reading His Word. Prayer is a love response of gratitude—a love exercised morning, noon, and night. Prayer's three purposes include bringing us to God, talking and listening to God, and providing a place to confront Satan in the presence of God. God answers prayers in three ways: Yes, No, Wait. Everybody wants the first answer but all too often receives the second or third. Why? God is not some glorified bellhop or elf to whom we give a Christmas list. Prayers are not always answered as we would like, because our requests are not in harmony with God's will (Matthew 6:10), because of disobedience (Deuteronomy 1:42–45), impatience (Hebrews 11:6), unconfessed sin (Psalm 66:16), or unbelief (Hebrews 11:6). But when we desire to know God, He is more than willing to reveal Himself to us. Hebrews 4:16 urges us to approach the throne of grace with confidence. James 1:6 admonishes us not to doubt. James 1:5 says to ask for wisdom.

Praying God's promises back to Him is a powerful weapon against Satan. If we read the holy prophets' prayers and how

God responded, then we can import their words into our own prayers. God is the same today as He was then. So many times I see books that claim to unlock the secrets of answered prayer. To me that concept is misguided! It sounds as if God is up there sitting on a box of blessings, unwilling to part with them unless one figures out the mystery or finds the key. The truth is all in the Bible, and it's not secret. It's plain as day and repeats itself over and over, but most are unwilling to take the necessary time to read and pray. What would happen if God paid as little attention to us as we pay to Him? Fortunately, He is long-suffering and so, so patient. It brings tears to my eyes when I think of all the times I spat on Him and cursed Him, yet He still held me close.

Some think it's hard to be saved. True, many are not going to be saved, not because it's hard but because they are unwilling to make the right decisions. The way is simple, the choice is easy, but many will not choose correctly. Why? Because they resist the Holy Spirit. They will not give in to His pleadings. Jesus died for ALL! Now if we will just believe in Him and stop fighting the Holy Spirit, we will be saved. We're already justified through Christ. It really truly is good news. Why be afraid? Be joyful in anticipation of the Second Coming!

Another concept is learned is the blessings of obedience. People wonder why their prayers aren't answered. Many times it's disobedience. In the Old Testament, obedience is rewarded with milk and honey. Disobedience brings famine and hardships. Salvation through faith is as solid as it gets. It is sad that so many slip into the ditch on either side of this golden offer. People in one ditch believe that a person can keep on sinning in the flesh because he or she is under grace. Those in the other ditch want to omit the grace and try in vain to earn that beautiful, free gift. Salvation is a gift through faith; gratitude responds with obedience out of love for the Author of our eternal life.

Patience is another key to successful living, and if a person didn't have patience when free, prison will force him to find some, especially during lockdowns. Several months passed before the administration attempted an unlock. After a lockdown ends, usually the victimized race retaliates to get even, or so they think. Sadly, the situation often deteriorates into an ongoing war. Paybacks seem to never end, but after eighteen months of tit-for-tat, our doors opened and the Mexicans and the Whites called a truce.

Shortly after that I was assigned the barber's job. Each race has its own barber, and God saw to it that I was given a job tailor-made for witnessing one-on-one. It became a standing joke on that yard that if anyone wanted a haircut—he'd get a sermon too. Amazingly, many of the most hardened convicts, when alone, one-on-one, would tell me of their belief in Jesus. But lacking courage and fearing retribution, they'd slip their masks of evil back on and disappear into the crowd.

Within a few months, Kenny was transferred to a less-violent yard. I'll forever cherish our time together, and I pray to be reunited in heaven. Sadness caused both of us to choke back tears, but God had a plan, and it wouldn't be stopped.

I immediately asked a new guy, a believer, to move in. Brian, a Pentecostal, was always ready for a good Bible study. We were both saddened by the lack of church services on our yard. Months would pass without sight of the chaplain or word of our little chapel doors opening. So one day God decided to do something about it and brought us along for the amazing ride.

My new celly, a charismatic Christian, loved to make his needs fully known to the Lord. He has blessed me, and I have learned much by praying with him and watching many requests being answered in full.

One day we had an unusually tall order for God and His mighty angels. Being in prison has its share of patience-growing moments. No doors open without keys and reasons—reasons deemed valid by the key holder who may be a grouchy guard looking for an excuse to say No. For the tasks we had in mind, we needed lots of open doors and no snarling guards.

We joined hands just before morning yard release, and Brian petitioned our Father in heaven, stating boldly that our church services had been neglected due to the many facility lockdowns and staff changes. He asked Jesus to open doors, grease the hinges, rebuke the devil, and pave the way to our chapel so we could worship Him. When he finished, I added "Amen," and out I went into the jungle called prison.

In my prison job as barber, I worked outside on the yard. I roamed around with my box of tools and cut hair inside the twenty-foot walls of our world. On the other side of that wall are the facility offices where a few inmates work as clerks and janitors. Normally it takes a written pass in order to enter, and also, an inmate must be dressed in full state blues, looking groomed and proper. Sergeants, lieutenants, and captains work there tending to the business at hand.

Dressed in my state blues, I went to the gate. When the tower cop asked what I wanted, I told him I was a Christian volunteer for the chapel. He eyed me up and down and pushed the button; the gate creaked open.

My heart pounded as I walked to the patio looking at all the office doors and picking one I thought would be best. Trying to look as if I worked there, I put my head down and entered. Inside I noticed three sergeants, a lieutenant, and several regular cops. Still moving, I saw at the back of a hallway an inmate working on a word processor in an office. I walked past the brass into the office. The inmate looked up, greeted me, and I returned his "hello" telling him I was the volunteer to get the Protestant church services up and running again. He shrugged and said OK.

Looking over his shoulder, I saw on the screen the names and housing locations of all the Asians who regularly attend Buddhist services. I asked him if he knew where the Protestant stuff might be, and he handed me a computer disk.

Oh great, I thought. *Computers. Mr. Ford's Introduction to Computers 101 in 1981 was the last time I'd sat in front of a computer screen. What now?*

The inmate probably assumed I knew how to operate the equipment, but as I stared at him with a "deer-caught-in-the-headlights" look, he motioned to a computer and said, "You can use that one."

I inserted the disk and followed the on-screen instructions. Up popped a screen full of files with all kinds of strange names, none of which looked like the Protestant church list. I swiveled my chair, looked my office mate in the eye, and said, "I'm lost and need a hand."

The inmate slid his chair over to my keyboard and in a flurry of taps brought up the master list. Not only did the disk have the master list of inmates who wanted to attend church; it also had all the forms and layouts needed to facilitate services. I sat in awe at the power of my Lord Jesus Christ. Of the entire maze of departments, offices, and cubicles, I had somehow walked straight into the one containing just the information I needed. But this was just the beginning. I sat at that desk and plinked and plunked those keys for hours without so much as a sideways glance from anyone. After editing and adding new names to the old list, I was finished.

My Buddhist friend told me I needed a copy for each of the buildings plus one for each gun tower and one for the sergeant. Now I felt nervous. I needed a sergeant to authorize copies and sign off on the whole list. None of the sergeants knew me, much less what I was doing.

Taking the original copy of the list, I headed for the sergeant's office, praying all the way. I gingerly tapped on the wall. Three pairs of eyes stared at me, and my throat felt dry, but the words came from somewhere. "I just need one of you fellas to give me your John Henry so I can get this list distributed to the buildings on time." The closest sergeant motioned for me to come in as he reached toward the papers I held. Once in the office, I felt like the last French fry on a plate. All three sergeants looked at me without speaking. As the closest man looked over the paperwork, I spoke. "Who gets copies and where do I get them?"

After signing the list, the sergeant motioned for a regular cop to step in. "You'll need twelve copies, and this officer will see that you get them."

I managed my thank-yous, turned, and followed the cop to another office complex, where he made twelve copies. My mind spun with the realization that I was in the middle of an amazing miracle. Nothing and nobody could stop what God was doing. Doors continued to open as if they were expected to!

Returning to the sergeant's office, I knew I still had a couple more hurdles to jump, but the Holy Spirit hadn't finished yet. Dropping off the sergeant's copy, I asked him when he'd like me back the next week. "Come Monday morning," he answered. "I'll get you sign-up sheets for all eight buildings so you can post them for the new guys. Oh, by the way, what's your name?"

"Fleck," I said over my shoulder while exiting the office. Talk about a pat on the back and a pass to do this all again the next week.

I gathered my copies, stuffed them into a folder, and as I headed back through the gauntlet of officers, I greeted them saying, "See you all on Monday." They glanced my way, nodded, and kept on talking. I wondered if some questioned, "Who is this guy? And why is he acting as if he works here?"

No matter—I work for a Boss who has a plan that never fails and whose door is always open.

Back I went through the big gate, past the twenty-foot wall, and into the yard. Going to each building, I handed out the lists so the staff would know whom to release for church.

When I finished, Brian came running to me frantically asking for a copy of the list. "I don't know if I have an extra one. Why?"

"The chaplain is on our yard on other business, and if he is going to hold the service, he has to have a copy of the list."

I found that I did have an extra, so he went running to let Chaplain Green know the list had been signed, and the guys would be at the service. If the chaplain had not been on our yard at just that time, he would not have known that the list had been approved and wouldn't have come to conduct services.

Sunday came and our little chapel was alive with men, a good turnout for the first service in several months. As the chaplain preached, the amens rang out. The following week we were locked down until Thursday. I feared it would be too late to get the list done because it's usually needed a few days before the weekend. I prayed God would help us again as He had in the past. My celly and I headed to the yard wondering how God would make this happen. No more than ten minutes had passed when I heard my name over the loudspeaker. "Inmate Fleck, report to the program office." I glanced at my celly, we both shouted "Amen!" and I ran off.

After changing into my state blues, I hurried toward the program office. Approaching the same tower cop as the previous week, I identified myself as Fleck, and he opened the door. I walked straight to the program office fully expecting to meet whoever had called, but nobody seemed to be expecting me. I had the creepy feeling I was being inspected. I went to the same small office where I had gone before, sat down, and started typing another list. When finished, I took it to the sergeant's office. Smiling, he scribbled his signature and motioned for his officer to make the appropriate copies.

My feet barely touched the ground as I left the building. The list had been on time for the second week, but the mystery of who called me remains unsolved. A few months passed, and our services grew wonderfully. The first list had twenty-five names. It grew to one hundred forty names. The chaplain announced that we had maxed the capacity of the chapel and must split into two services. I couldn't think of a better problem.

Next we selected elders for our congregation. The men wanted Bibles, spiritual books, and Bible studies. They voiced prayer requests. Two building officers stopped me one day and asked why so many guys suddenly wanted to attend Protestant services. I responded, "Do you believe in God?"

"Yes," they both responded.

"Good. Sit back and watch His hand work miracles. We're having a revival!" The chain of events that fell into place is nothing short of amazing. I dare anyone to call it a coincidence. When I look back at the many hurdles we overcame, I feel dizzy.

So many times we defeat God's work because we fail to take that leap of faith. We look to the future and become discouraged. The path seems too steep, the rocks too jagged, the air too thin. Jesus says, " 'I will do whatever you ask in my name, so that the Son may bring glory to the Father. You may ask me for anything in my name, and I will do it' " (John 14:13, 14).

Many times in the past eight years of incarceration I've asked Why? At times like this when God's hand is almost tangible, His face almost visible, I know why. There is no mountain He will not move if we trust in Him.

Chapter 28

SALTY

With our church-service attendance filling the chapel, a few of us brothers discussed the possibility of starting a discipleship group that would be responsible for meeting the needs of the many members. Basing it on the guidelines set forth in Timothy and Titus, we sent a proposal to the head chaplain, hoping to have a solid nucleus of dedicated Christians who could meet once a week in the chapel. During this meeting we would bring requests to the Lord in prayer, sing praises, and have a different brother each week give a message from the Bible.

Before long we received approval, and our discipleship meetings began. Our first meeting had twelve men—we didn't miss the irony. Soon it grew to thirty, and baptisms resulted. What an unforgettable sight to see grown men plastered with tattoos being baptized. A person might wonder if church was the right place for them. But seeing their beaming, tear-filled faces upon rising from the chilly water, we knew the Spirit dwelt within. Drug dealers, robbers, murderers, and all kinds of formerly extremely evil men were now cleansed and ready to put in work for Jesus. A man named Salty was one of them.

He introduced himself as Salty. Salty? I'd never heard of him. He looked late forties, about five feet six inches, quite heavy for his height, and rather stressed out, as are all new inmates after a long bus ride. "Do you need anything?" I asked.

"I need a smoke."

"Sorry, I don't smoke. But if you need soap, toothpaste, or something to read, I can help you there."

His eyes lit up and his face beamed. "I'm a Christian, too, and I could really use a Bible right now." We talked for a minute, and then I returned to my cell. He seemed sort of an odd fellow, but I couldn't get past his genuineness, something not often seen in prison because most wear masks to hide fears and the past.

We occasionally saw each other and met in church. Every week he'd be right there in front, praising the Lord. A few months later when the chaplain organized a baptism, fourteen guys decided to make their commitment public, and Salty was one of them.

Later the prison officials did a massive move of inmates to another yard, taking my celly along with Salty's celly and many others. This is a situation that no one in prison enjoys, and an inmate has basically two choices: either find someone ASAP who will move in or just wait and hope that whoever comes through that door is compatible. Due to overcrowding, bed spaces fill up immediately.

Living side by side can be hard even with someone I like, so while praying that evening, I wondered whom God would put in my cell. The next morning I started thinking about Salty but hesitated because of the smoking. I had lived with smokers before and preferred not to. But Salty and I would have Christ in common, and that's what matters.

The more I thought about it, the more I felt impressed to give him a shout. Kneeling again, I asked God to lead, rose from my knees, went to the door, and yelled down the tier, "Salty!"

"Yes, Skip?"

"Hey, do you want to move up here with me?"

After a pause came a healthy holler, "Yes, positively!"

So there it was—Salty was moving in. After putting down his belongings, he said, "I'm going to quit smoking." Having quit myself years earlier, I knew how hard it is to break an addiction, but I hoped he could do it. He seemed determined.

Weeks rolled by, and not only did Salty kick the habit, but he began to exercise. Weighing well over 220 pounds, he had a mountainous task. The resolution that I saw with breaking the tobacco habit, I now saw with the exercise. But the best part was studying the Bible together. Salty already had knowledge of God but still had many questions needing answers. He loved the Lord with all his heart and showed it every time we'd do our studies. He also told me of disappointing previous years in Salinas Valley Prison. For five years he'd been trying to get moved to Folsom, where most of his family lived. His mother had had several heart surgeries, his father battled cancer, and both were elderly. Naturally Salty prayed and pleaded with God to be transferred to a prison close enough for them to visit. He begged his counselor to send him south, anywhere except High Desert Prison, far from his family.

I wondered what God had in store for Salty, and we prayed time and time again for God's will to be revealed. As months melted away, I still didn't know why God had sent Salty to High Desert, but one thing was certain: Salty was a work in progress. His conviction to get in shape and kick the habit paid big dividends. In about ten months he weighed 170 pounds, ran four miles a day, and looked like a new man. Even the staff commented on the new and improved Salty McGraw. The guys started calling him "Slim," making his eyes gleam and an ear-to-ear smile pop out. But in the quiet time of cell living, he still questioned, "Why High Desert?"

With spring came news of his father's declining health. All of the Christian brothers banded together in prayer sessions asking for mercy and healing for Ray McGraw.

Ray McGraw had come to know the Lord at age eight in Jacksonville, Florida, and a local pastor of the Southern Baptist Church baptized him. Shortly after his baptism, while playing with a boy named Harry in a vacant lot, Ray began telling him about a book in heaven with many names. Then he explained his newly found love for the Lord and his assurance of salvation through Christ. One can only imagine how two eight-year-old Southern boys discussed the plan of salvation, but Ray's words had a life-changing effect on Harry. The following weekend Harry asked the pastor for baptism. After Bible studies, Harry was baptized. When he turned thirteen, Harry decided to be a preacher. Then Ray and Harry lost track of each other for the next fifty-plus years, but Harry always wondered what had become of Ray and his brother Joe. Years later Harry preached at the old church in Jacksonville and told of his conversion experience in the vacant lot. As he thought of the true favor Ray had done for him, he wondered if he could ever repay Ray for his heartfelt testimony that long-ago day.

Spring came late to High Desert, and as Chaplain Green drove to prison, smells of the sage and fresh grass permeated the air. He picked up his keys at the front gate and walked to his office to review the previous day's voicemail messages. Being the head chaplain has its benefits, but it also comes with the undesirable task of notifying inmates of lost loved ones. When the chaplain pushed play, a woman's voice explained that her late husband's son was housed at High Desert and asked the chaplain to notify him that his father had passed away. She left her name and number, so Chaplain Green called to express his condolences. The woman said her husband's name was Ray McGraw, and she had just returned from Jacksonville, Florida, where she'd buried him at the Riverview Baptist Church on Lem Turner Road.

The old chaplain was silent for a moment and then asked, "Do you know a man named Joe McGraw?"

"Why, of course. That was Ray's brother."

Chaplain Green quietly let the unbelievable news sink in. They chatted for a few more minutes. Then, hanging up the phone, the chaplain grabbed his wide-brimmed plantation hat and headed for C yard.

When the door opened to our cell and the tower cop told Salty to get up and go to the program office, neither of us knew why. But when told to report to program, nobody hesitates. Arriving at the office, Salty met the silvery-haired Southern Baptist chaplain. Telling Salty to sit down, Chaplain Green looked into his eyes and recognized the resemblance of an old friend from many years ago. Saying "Mr. McGraw," in that unmistakable Southern drawl to which only Chaplain Green can do justice, he asked, "Is your daddy Ray McGraw?"

"Yes," said Salty.

"Did he have a brother named Joe?"

"Yes."

Tears began to well up in the old preacher's deep-blue eyes. He told Salty of the passing of his father. The tears stayed as he continued to relive the wonderful story of how sixty-three years before, in a vacant lot on a hot Florida afternoon, a young man had given him the news of salvation. Chaplain Harry Green had never thought in his wildest imagination there would come a day when he could repay his boyhood friend, Ray McGraw, the favor. He told Salty, "You have a friend for life."

Salty returned to our cell and after a few minutes of sitting in amazement mixed with grief, he told me the whole saga. When he finished, neither of us wondered why God had allowed him to be transferred to High Desert rather than Folsom. Since coming here, Salty had given his life fully to God and publicly declared it with baptism. He'd lost more than fifty pounds, given up smoking, and become a walking example of how God works.

Although the death of his father has been hard, Salty knows he'll see him again. Chaplain Green's amazing testimony shows how closely our heavenly Father knows and cares for each of us. Salty now had a friend for life in the old Southern chaplain with the wide-brimmed hat, and I truly believe this amazing twist of fate has put a spark back in Harry's life too.

Chaplain Green says he's never seen such a miracle in all his years and says also, "I do not know what the future holds, but I know who holds the future."

Chapter 29

NO SUCH THING
AS "NO"

Granted—the Lord was doing some powerful things on our yard. Many men came to know Jesus, and their lives appeared even more miraculous when viewed alongside the overwhelming violence of daily living. We seemed to live in a bubble that floated around the yard, existing in a safe place surrounded by ferocious evil.

One week had been especially rough. Four guys had been stabbed, one a Christian brother, an ex-gang member. All I could do was pray for him. I spoke to him moments after the stabbing, and rather than being angry, he was grateful for God's hand of protection. I don't know why he got it, but many times gang members have closets full of past deeds, and, obviously, somebody figured he had to go. My celly and I had special prayer for all four; fortunately, no one died.

I was ready for a change—these experiences are very traumatic, and I felt that over the years I had become desensitized to the seriousness of this life—perhaps like being in a war zone, an observer, yet right in the middle of the drama. On the upside, the constant uncertainty of what lay ahead kept me on my knees with my hand tightly grasping the hem of Jesus' robe for deliverance.

Each time I heard of an inmate about to be stabbed, I'd run to the Lord and plead on his behalf. Often he'd be spared serious injury, but not always. One day the devil turned his ugly head my way, forcing me to make a decision that could have been deadly.

When I first heard about prison politics, I snickered to myself. What could these uneducated gangsters know about politics? Obviously the politics of prison would be very different from the streets. Here, bad choices can be life ending, not just career threatening. Having never been on a level-four maximum security prison made me a fish, or rather a guppy, in the sea of sharks—sharks that endlessly roam about searching an opportunity to prey and kill. I was the greenest of guppies.

The vast California prison system inters 150,000 inmates in fifty-plus prisons classified in four major categories called levels. Inmates with little time—no more than a year or two—who have committed no violent offenses, start prison life on level one.

Lethal electric fences surround level-two prisons, making escape unlikely. For the most part, they are filled with petty criminals, although some lifers who've been incarcerated for fifteen or more years may be lucky enough to live there. Chuckawalla was one of these.

In level three the situation begins to get serious because many lifers and serious criminals inhabit these yards. Guards have guns in the towers, and they aren't afraid to use them. But most of the guys on level three, although serious criminals, have decided to follow the rules unless something major happens that might force a man's hand and cause him to react violently.

The most violent yards, level four, are war zones made up of men who have nothing to lose. Most are lifers, and in California, a life sentence means life—not twenty or thirty or forty years. Life sentences in some other states may mean twenty-five or thirty years to life, but nobody in California with an "L" on his sentence is getting out. I've met men who were given seven years to life sentences thirty years ago, and no parole awaits them.

This situation breeds violence because inmates have no incentive to be good or "program," as it's called inside. In level-four prisons live the worst of the worst; a smile rarely means "Have a nice day" or "See ya later." Hard, cold, tattooed machines circle the track in pairs or packs for protection. Although I have no tattoos to speak of, and the coldest thing on me is my forehead in winter, I call this environment home.

Every yard has a hierarchy of inmates, a basic dictatorship made up of men who have earned respect by force. Each race has its own governing body with a "shot-caller" who aligns himself with the Who's Who on the yard. He's self-appointed and just assumes his position, depending on how long he's been in prison and whom he knows. I've seen some shot-callers who hang in the shadows letting their henchmen or homeboys carry out their orders; other chiefs stand out and rule with authority and presence.

Inevitably shot-callers leave the yard. They call a shot for someone to be stabbed, and often the victim will tell the staff who called the shot. If the charge can be proved, the shot-caller and "shooter," along with the victim, depart. On our yard, henchmen enforced a "no hands" policy because no fistfighting is tolerated. All problems are to be solved with weapons. This sounds crazy, but it does have a point (excuse the pun). If two men get upset with each other, they know there's only one way to handle it. If they stab each other, they'll both go to Pelican Bay for at least eighteen months of total segregation from the general population. The "no hands" policy forces men to bite their tongues and think before they speak. But the flip side of the coin is that somebody who can't stay on the yard for any one of many reasons, ranging from being a rat or snitch to convictions for rape, baby killing, and child molestation, becomes a victim and potentially could die from a stabbing.

The minute a new inmate arrives, he must produce his paper-work stating the charges. These identify his crime, and if he's not one of the above, he can stay. Also, a new inmate is asked how much time he has and if he's ever "put in work," the dreaded three words that send chills down a first-termer's spine. "Putting in work" is the lingo used to describe cleaning up a yard. Those offenses listed previously carry a death sentence and need indi-viduals called shooters to exact punishment. As a first-termer with a life sentence, I fit the criteria of a shooter. This potential assignment frightened me, and whenever I heard of an upcom-ing hit on an unsuspecting person who had a bad "jacket" or charge, I'd get nervous. I knew the guys would be looking for a shooter to stab the victim. Oftentimes youngsters raised their hands and volunteered to put in work as a rite of passage and being looked upon as a solid homeboy who could be counted on.

I always felt confused because only one out of a hundred would actually get away with the stabbing, so as soon as the assault took place, the shooter and victim would disappear, one to the infirmary, the other to Pelican Bay and then down the road to wherever. So why would a man stab another man if he had nothing against him? It was all about intimidation and fear.

As a Christian, I knew I had no business ever picking up a weapon for any reason, but I also knew the shot-caller would not hesitate to ask me. Not wanting to look weak and fearing retri-bution, I always prayed earnestly that God would protect me and that no one would ask me to put in work. Always someone would volunteer, and I'd breathe more easily and thank God. But I didn't realize that perfect love casts out fear, and I should have been ready and waiting to stand up for God by rebuking the sharks as they exacted their manipulative politics. I tried to make friends with the current shot-caller, hoping he would rec-ognize that I wasn't in the mix and had nothing to do with politics. I guess that'd be my own politicking—trying to align myself with the one who'd make the final decision on who must pick up the knife and run it into a victim.

One day the shot-caller stopped by my door. I'd heard he was looking for a shooter, and my heart skipped as he crowded up to the crack in my door and began to whisper, so instead of listening to him, I asked if he knew the Lord. This question came straight out of left field, and by his look, he was shocked. My knees shook, but without letting him speak, I began to tell him I had some good Christian books for him to read if he wanted them. I paused as a bewildered face looked at me, and he sputtered, "No thank you. I'm cool on the books," and walked off.

I rejoiced, thanking God. The shot-caller understood I had no desire to get involved in anything but God's business and left to find another less talkative guppy. *Whew!* I thought, *That was close.* I didn't have to say No, I didn't have to look weak, and he'd not be back to ask me again. One day, quite unexpectedly, guards took that caller from our yard and, like many times before, there would soon be a new sheriff in town.

In this way a young man named Red chose to run our yard. He'd recently completed a six-year stay in the segregated housing units on Pelican Bay, a lonesome place designed for those so violent they can't even be on a level-four yard. When a stabbing or killing happens in prison, the shooter or assailant gets sent to Pelican Bay for six months to six years or even an indeterminate time if the system deems such appropriate. A simple stabbing usually rates eighteen months.

Red had just completed six years at the Bay, so I could imagine the active violence in which he had been involved. When he first arrived in our yard, he looked a bit shell-shocked by all the movement: inmates walking the track, playing sports, running here and there. At Pelican Bay he would have spent most of his time alone, and the rare times he left the cell, he'd be shackled hand and foot with two short-tempered cops escorting him. Soon, though, he began to assimilate, with a smile and hand-shake ready for everyone. His respectful demeanor seemed to contradict his past, but nobody made any attempt to test his kindness, knowing where he'd come from and why.

Because I then cut hair on the yard, I first met Red when he needed a haircut. About every three weeks he'd find me, and I always had time for Red.

Red had been on the yard about a year, and his walk spoke volumes about his commitment to maintain his authority. He militantly redefined what he expected: "There is no such thing as No. If you have fifteen years or more to do, you will be considered active and willing to participate in any request involving putting in work. No one is exempt."

"There is no such thing as saying No" was the mantra that rolled over the yard among the eligible. Anyone deciding to say No would be put into the category of victim and dealt with accordingly. I immediately found my closest Christian brother, and we prayed and pleaded with God to change this policy or protect us in some way. Within the next week or two, several guys who fit the criteria decided to tell the cops that they feared for their lives, and one by one they disappeared. I also thought about going out as a coward, but how would that glorify God? My Christian brother and I decided to stay, but the decision troubled me when fear would attack. I'd seen many stabbings and knew that the victim usually didn't see it coming. I'd walk the yard wondering if today was my day—the devil would instantly spot the fear and begin stretching, pushing, and pulling on my imagination.

One day, while playing handball, I noticed Red waiting on the sidelines. Instantly my mind began rolling with thoughts of *What now? What if?* As soon as I finished playing, Red walked over, shook my hand, and asked to talk to me. I knew the time had come for me to put up or shut up for Christ. A thousand thoughts raced through my mind. *Does he have a shooter waiting in the crowd ready to take my life if I say No? Will he be the shooter? Does he have a knife on him? Oh, Lord, please come to my rescue.*

I told Red, "Sure, I have a few minutes for you. Could we walk some laps as we talk?" He agreed, and off we went. I felt weird walking with him, knowing what he was capable of doing and realizing the time had come. He began saying he had the keys, another way of identifying him as the shot-caller. And in the prison yard, Red did have the keys; but praise God, He holds my keys. As Red spoke, I listened and a sense of calm came over me. I decided to stand up for Christ but had no idea how or if I could finish before being attacked. Red explained the militant policy and reasons for it. In the past Christians had been given a bad name because they used the Bible as a shield from attackers. Child molesters and the like had claimed Christianity to avoid questions, and guppies who fit the shooter criteria also had claimed to be Christian in hopes of an exemption from the task at hand. Sadly, these men are exposed quickly and dealt with even more harshly than most. But their dishonesty casts a bad light and questions the validity of those who truly serve God. So to prevent any of the half-stepping, nobody is considered exempt.

Red paused, and I knew I must speak. My first words were choked up as my mouth went dry as sawdust, but I stumbled on. "Red," I said, "I respect you and understand your reasons and methods for running this yard. I know where I am; I'm in prison on a very serious yard, and issues I am not involved in need to be dealt with. Red, you know I'm a Christian. I pray for you and all the men that someday you'll come to know Jesus as I do. He died for you, and you will have to answer to Him someday, as will I. Red, I mean no disrespect as I tell you I humbly refuse to take part in any of the politics that occur on this yard. That is my stand, and I am willing to accept any punishment that may come with my decision."

Silence for a few moments—I could feel the prickly sensation of sweat rolling down my back. *Is it time? Is it now? What is it going to feel like?* These thoughts raced through my mind as Satan attacked me with fear. Then in a low, closely guarded voice, Red began to speak. "Skip, I've seen you and know that you're not hiding behind the Bible. Yet I have made this rule to stop anyone from sliding by without having to put in work. I'll tell you what I'll do. Since it's me who has the final decision on who does the stabbing, I'll give you my word that I won't ask you. But you have to promise me you'll not mention this to anyone, or there will be trouble." I was silent. He continued, "I understand your position, and everything will be cool."

Just then the Spirit nudged me, and I again spoke out. "Red, my Christian brother Dirk is also in the same position as I, so if it's possible . . ." my voice trailed off as Red looked at me with his deadly stare. "OK, then, just you two. That's it." He stuck out his hand. I shook it like a slave being given his freedom papers.

"Thank You, God. Praise You, Jesus," I said over and over.

About three weeks later Red and seven of his accomplices were escorted off the yard, not to be seen again. And like many times before, the cycle had once again begun. There would be a new sheriff in town. I'd have to make another stand. Praise God!

Chapter 30

THE

LETTER

Aman named Bill, whom I mentioned earlier, played a unique part in my life, and by the grace of God, I played a part in his after my incarceration. This story unfolded over twenty years. Praise God for continuing to throw lifelines of faith through answered prayer.

Although very nervous when I first had begun pitching, I was excited about my new job demonstrating a juice maker at fairs and exhibitions, the first one of which was scheduled to begin in two days. My boss, Walter, had me at the booth practicing. Shaking in my shoes, I stumbled and fumbled through pitch after pitch, trying to get the spiel right.

Glancing to my left, I noticed two middle-aged gentlemen approaching the booth and stopping directly in front of my counter. Pretending not to see them, I continued to talk. Suddenly one of the men grabbed a raw egg and plopped it into the blender, instantly covering me with sticky goop. As I backed up, I saw a covertly hidden group laughing hysterically at my now splattered clothes. With my face turned pink and ears burning red, I heard a hearty, "Welcome to the business, Rick. My name's Bill Latoski."

His light-blue opalescent eyes and flashing smile instantly conveyed an air of confidence and invincibility. The crowd continued chuckling as I attempted to shake Bill's hand, realizing I'd been the target of an initiation ritual, a practical joke played on all rookies.

Watching Bill as he walked away, I schemed about getting even for the humiliation, but a hand touched my shoulder, and my boss said, "You'll have to get up pretty early in the morning to get ole Bill. He's been doing this since he was your age." Bill, a veteran cookware salesman who owned his company, was undoubtedly the most charismatic man I'd ever met, and he seemed filled with almost superhuman energy.

I took to the pitch business like a gnat to flypaper and began to hang around Bill's booth. He'd invite me to listen to his pitch and then give little pointers on how to sell and close a deal. His uncanny ability to spot the ready buyers and coax a large check from their pockets mesmerized me. Often he'd wink at me as if to say, "Watch this, Kid. I'm closing another deal." I imagined selling cookware, too, and doing it just like Bill.

The pitch business is one of constant hype, and a salesman must be excited about selling. While a few people like Bill have that natural ability, most don't, so some turn to drugs. Unfortunately, I chose drugs for motivation. As years passed, I sank deeper into addictions. I always showed up for work, although rarely sober.

One morning after a night of partying, I sipped coffee in my booth hoping to find alertness in the black liquid. I hadn't slept for days and didn't want to see anyone. Suddenly, there he was, eyes still blue but terrifyingly piercing. He stared for a moment, gazing intently at his former rosy-cheeked, bright-eyed protégé. Motioning for me to follow, he walked to the back of the exhibition hall. Suddenly he swung around, brought his face inches from mine, and spent a few minutes explaining the facts of life to a once cocky but now terrified young man. Bill hated drugs. He'd seen men become mice because of drugs, and now seeing me throwing my whole life and potential away made him insanely angry.

When he walked away, I wept. I knew he was right, and he cared enough to say words that burrowed deep into my numbed mind. I wasn't fooling anyone. I wasn't selling much, and I was miserable. A couple of days later, my boss fired me, and after some counseling, I checked into drug rehab. Unfortunately sobriety continued to elude me until I was incarcerated.

After a miracle of being "born again," I began to walk in the light and mercy of my Lord and Savior. Occasionally, during the years of incarceration, I'd get a card or letter from Bill, always bursting with energy and life. But then came a different type of letter sent by a friend in the business telling of Bill's sudden and serious illness. How could this be? Not Bill, not the guy with the Midas touch. The letter contained details of the cancer that had abruptly changed the life of my wealthy friend. He'd been vibrant, full of life. He'd made millions and traveled around the globe enjoying everything this world has to offer. But now, sitting on his veranda in a wheelchair, he watched his life ebb away. The news devastated me. Feeling helpless, I asked God, *What can I do?*

I prayed to God, asking Him to speak to Bill, to give him another chance at life, and, infinitely more important, eternal life. Then a Voice spoke from the depths of my prayer, *Write to him.* I ignored the impression but continued in prayer. *Write to him and tell him about Me,* the Voice insisted. I obeyed and wrote, reminding Bill of the day he had read me the riot act for using drugs, of how I looked up to and was inspired by him. Then I changed gears and wrote, "Bill, just like you did so many years ago for me, I'm going to tell you something of life-and-death importance.

"Jesus Christ is real, Bill. He reached down into the quagmire of lost souls and pulled me out. He is my Savior and waits to be yours too. Bill, you've seen, had, and tasted all the world has to offer, and today you are in a strangely enviable position that most people don't experience. You know you have only a few weeks left on this earth, so why not give your life to Jesus? What do you have to lose? You never said No to a good deal, and I don't think you'll find a better one than this. Jesus died for you, and now He's waiting for you to believe in Him."

After I wrote a bit more, I closed telling him I'd meet him on the streets paved with gold. I shed tears writing the letter hoping they'd be rewarded by the miracle of Bill's salvation.

Two weeks later a friend relayed the sad news of Bill's passing and mentioned the letter. It had arrived the day before Bill's death, and his wife read it to him, but because of the medication and the ravages of the disease, she wasn't sure he'd understood. My heart fell—the letter was too late. "But," the voice on the line continued, "over two hundred people heard your words when Shirley, Bill's wife, read the letter at his funeral. There wasn't a dry eye in the church that day at this secular funeral, and they all heard the appeal of an inmate doing a life sentence a thousand miles away."

I learned that when you hear God's voice telling you to act, don't hesitate. God's timing is always perfect.

Chapter 31

A MIRACLE ENTITLED "PRO BONO"

W ith 2002 coming to a close, yet another miracle would soon unfold. Four years had passed since that dreadful day of the verdict. Prison had become a way of life, and each sunrise brought evidence of God's mighty hand working to further *His* plan.

One evening right after chow, a guard showed up at my door with legal mail. Legal mail is distributed separately from regular mail. Staff reads and inspects all regular mail such as letters, postcards, and periodicals, but they bring legal mail to our doors sealed. With staff watching closely, we open and display the contents briefly, showing them there's no contraband. For confidentiality purposes, staff cannot read our unopened legal mail.

I held my breath as I noticed the return address—the attorney general's office. For years I'd been waiting for the final response from the state on my appeal, and this was it. Nervously I opened the packet, fanned through the paperwork to satisfy the officer, who then turned on his heels and disappeared. Heart pounding, I held what could be my ticket to freedom. I said a silent prayer and turned to the back page.

A sudden flood of anger mixed with despair shot through me. *Denied.* I folded the brief shut and stuffed it deep into my locker, covering it with every paper I could find. Sobbing, I lay down pleading with God, asking, *Why, Lord, why, did You miraculously grant twenty-five thousand dollars, only to crush my hopes after all these years? You paid for my lawyer, and now the appeal is denied. How is that possible?* I continued in accusatory prayer not realizing my shortsightedness.

A day later I called my parents, but even though they were also shaken by the news, they encouraged me to take heart. They explained that my lawyer would be up to see me shortly.

A few weeks later he arrived, and an officer escorted me to the visiting area for our meeting. Bill Kopeny reminded me of my first lawyer, as both looked elegant and confident. Bill greeted me with a smile and introduced me to his assistant, Kelly. Four years earlier Bill had been hired with miracle funds, but now it seemed to me that we were no further ahead and possibly further behind than when we started. At least back then I still had a chance. Today the future looked hopeless.

But Bill radiated energy with no apparent sign of defeat. Staring at him, I felt anger. *Lawyers,* I thought with a twinge of disgust. *Sharks, worse than the ones I deal with every day on the yard. Cunning, merciless, and life-sucking, always looking for a new opening to exploit and extract money from desperate people ignorant of the laws.* Satan attacked me in force, and I began falling into his trap. With my jaw set, I greeted him with a curt "Hello." And no small talk.

Smiling, he tried to lighten the mood saying, "You look healthy. It's good to see you again." I didn't bite, remaining stoic, wondering *What now?*

"Look, Rick," he began. "We're in a good position. The judges who heard your appeal didn't unanimously agree on your denial. It takes two of the three judges to uphold the conviction in order to deny your appeal. Usually at the state level of direct appeal, all three will turn you down." He took a breath, then continued. I remained silent, but a faint ray of hope flickered in the shadow of my mind. "Few appeals at this level get over-turned. We pretty much knew the direct appeal wasn't going to get it done. . . ."

His words faded. I felt anger rising in my throat. "Most cases are overturned at the federal level to which the state appeal is a precursor." He must have sensed my anger. Moving closer in his seat and lowering his voice he said, "We need to continue this, Rick. You have a good chance, and I believe we can win."

With those words my anger melted. I must have been looking for an opening in the horrible reality, and it appeared through his silky-soft words. "OK, Bill," I said. "What do we need to do?"

He slowly sat back, knowing he'd rekindled my shattered faith in him. "Rick, we need to go ahead with the writ of habeas corpus, which will encompass everything that didn't get heard in your trial. Once we put it together, we'll submit it with the di-rect appeal to the federal court, which is where you have the best chance of winning."

I sat taking it all in, wondering how long and how much more money would be needed. "All right, Bill. How much more money do you need?" I said flatly in my best business voice.

Bill looked at his assistant, then back at me, saying nothing. I braced myself for the amount, but he said nothing. "Look, Bill." I began softly clearing my throat. "I don't know if you're aware of how your initial fee of twenty-five thousand dollars was raised or where it came from."

"Well, I understand some friends helped you out."

"Oh, Bill, it was much more than that. You told us your fee, and we began praying for that amount. Two weeks later God provided it in full." My voice, now strong and full of conviction, stated, "Bill, I need to know your full amount, exactly how much is all this going to cost?"

He looked uneasy, eyes darting to and fro, not wanting to commit. Once again I said, "How much?"

"Ten thousand dollars for the habeas corpus and another five thousand for the federal appeal."

I sat back. "Fifteen thousand dollars, Bill. Is that the final tab?"

"Yep," he replied almost sheepishly. "You can ask God for fifteen thousand dollars."

I stared at him and wondered what he was thinking. *Fifteen thousand, from God?* It probably sounded almost cynical to him. But I knew God would provide. Saying goodbye, I returned to my cell and on my knees asked God, *What now?*

"Yep, Mom, Dad, he said fifteen thousand would take it to the federal court where I would stand the best chance of winning." I hung up the phone hoping the news hadn't devastated them. We decided, once again, to tell no one of the amount. Only God would know, and the money would be a clear sign from Him as to my future. I prayed, *Lord, if You plan on someday allowing me to walk free from this place, then please supply the dollars. But if it's Your will that I spend the rest of my life in prison, then so be it. I only request that You also give me the strength to handle Your decision.*

One month, then two, three, and four sped by without so much as a hint of anyone offering to help our financial need. Had God decided to say No? Often Satan badgered me with doubt, but the Holy Spirit would flash James 1:6 in my mind. *"When he asks, he must believe and not doubt. . . ."* And because of what He'd already done, I had confidence He would do it again.

One day a letter arrived from my lawyer announcing he'd be coming to see me soon. With no funds in sight, I prayed even harder, but with each day disappearing and no money forthcoming, I began to fear the worst. God had been so quick to supply the funds at the beginning. *Why doesn't He hear me now?* I questioned.

Ten months passed, and I sat once again across from Bill and Kelly. Feeling dejected, knowing this might be the last time we met, I forced a smile. With no funds, this meeting could end quickly. My trust in lawyers had been crushed over the years, making me view them with contempt, but today I sat helplessly at Bill's mercy, pleading silently for God to perform a miracle.

As soon as the greetings were out of the way, Bill started. "Rick, we're doing good. I've got some ideas, and we need to get on them."

Stopping him midsentence, I said, "Bill, hold on a minute." He paused, took a breath, and stared at me. *The time has come to call it a day,* I thought. *No money means no lawyer, and I don't want to waste his time.* "Bill, we don't have the money and can't afford your services anymore."

The words sounded so final; I wished I could take them back. Nothing but silence followed, neither of us saying anything. He looked at me, then at his assistant, then back at me. Sliding slightly forward in his seat, he lowered his voice once again. Looking me straight in the eyes, he began, "Rick, I know you can't afford my services. I know your parents don't have the means by which to pay my fee." He paused and looked at Kelly again. She nodded, and he continued. "But, Rick, you can't afford not to continue. We can win this, and that's why I've decided to take the case pro bono."

Pro bono—the words took my breath away. A surge of hope instantly rushed through my body. "Excuse me," I sputtered. "Did you say 'pro bono'?"

"Yes, Rick, I'll waive my fee." He sat back in his seat, letting the weight of his words take me. I sat in shock wondering if this was a dream. "Oh, my Lord and my God, I believe!" With tears brimming in my eyes, I still did not fully comprehend the miracle God had just performed. Calloused by lawyers from the past, I tried as I might to find the angle, the reason for Bill's generosity, but found no angle, no hidden agenda. "OK, Bill," I began, "what if one of my issues is granted, and I need you to appear in court. Isn't there an additional fee for that court appearance?"

"Yes, there is, and it's covered. Rick, I will cover you all the way through. There will be no charge. I know it's fine with you, but I want you to talk to your parents. I don't want to disrespect them, so if they want to give me something, it's fine. But I don't need your money. I have plenty."

I stood and shook Bill's hand, thanking him again and again. Tears brimming, I said Goodbye. Once back in my cell, all the emotion came flooding out as I fell to my knees in praise and thanks to my precious Lord. Another lifeline. Another building block of faith.

Chapter 32

RACISM AND
RIOTS

Growing up on a farm in western Canada sheltered me from the vile reality of true racism. My parents had taught me that all people are created equal, and I remember singing the words, "Red and yellow, black and white, all are precious in His sight. Jesus loves the little children of the world," from the song "Jesus Loves the Little Children." Our church congregation, as well as our community, had several minority families, but I never saw them as anything other than neighbors and friends.

When I began working in the United States, I noticed some racial divisions, depending on the geographical area, but nothing prepared me for the hatred inside prison walls. This hatred is hinted at as soon as a person gets off the bus into reception. He is asked to fill out some paperwork: addresses to next of kin, date of birth, citizenship, and race or ethnicity. Once the inmate checks the box applicable to race, the staff asks, "Who do you associate with?" If White, then the next questions will involve subgroups, gangs such as skinheads, who generally hate anyone non-White. But their worst enemy in prison would probably be another White gang called the Nazi Low Riders. Archenemies, they will fight immediately if given the opportunity. They have a standing "on sight" policy, which means, upon seeing a rival, they must attack. Among the other White gangs, the most infamous is the Aryan Brotherhood, or AB as they are commonly called inside. Undoubtedly the most feared, ABs have been plucked off mainline yards and now are kept in special housing units, having no contact with anyone else.

The Blacks have even more divisions, such as the Crips, the Bloods, and the BGFs, or Black Guerilla Family. Crips' color is blue, Bloods' is red, and on the streets they're mortal enemies. In prison they coexist, although they will not be housed in the same cell with each other. The Hispanics have two major divisions: Sureños and Norteños (southsiders and northsiders). The Southsiders' number is 13 and the Northsiders fly the number 14. South is blue, North is red, and they hate each other inside and outside. Riots often erupt between the two.

Other groups too numerous to mention exist, but these are the main ones, and most riots with serious consequences involve any two or more of those listed. Whites are generally allied with the Southsiders, although it's not uncommon to see the two riot. Blacks and Northsiders usually are allies, although they'll go at it too. But the bitterest rivals are the Blacks and the Whites. California is one of a handful of states that segregate by race. Each race can "cell up" or live only with another person of his own affiliation. This separation adds fuel to the racial hotbed. Each yard has sets of tables, exercise bars, and handball and basketball courts. Each race has its own tables, bars, and often courts too, another enabler forming racial barriers.

Whether the segregating is done to avoid problems or to redirect hostility, keeping the hatred between races and off officers, is a subject debated daily. The answer to that question remains elusive, but the reality is that racism is the most deadly force in prison. Among inmates the issue becomes even more defined. Whites are given the convict codes of racial interaction immediately upon arriving. Whites cannot eat, smoke, or drink after any other group except their allies, the Southern Mexicans. They can't play cards or games with anyone except allies. Peer pressure keeps association with rivals at a minimum.

As a Christian inmate, I've felt the piercing eyes and caught the sideways glances of men as I shake hands and often hug my non-White brothers. I have always praised God for the latitude He has provided me to witness to all races while under the watchful, hateful eyes of many. Coexisting in this environment of extreme hate inevitably leads to violence on a large scale. With the boiling point only a degree away, the tiniest problem can cause devastating mayhem. Unpaid drug debts, disrespect, or even a couple of missing cassette tapes can set off a riot.

The Bible promise " 'No weapon forged against you will prevail' " (Isaiah 54:17) is scrawled on a worn strip of paper kept deep in my pocket. A few years ago I had decided to make this promise my weapon of choice because prison is obviously a dangerous place, especially on the maximum-security yard I call home. Frequently inmates carry improvised weapons and don't hesitate to use them. Races hate each other, making violence and riots the norm, not the exception.

On a warm September day, our cell doors finally had squeaked open, marking the end of a four-month lockdown following a violent racial riot. This riot, initiated by the Whites, didn't happen on my yard, but the possibility of retaliation, called a ripple effect, caused the warden to shut down all movement and programs. During a lockdown, which can last from a few days to a couple of years, depending on the situation, inmates are confined to cells. Prison authorities hope that tempers will cool and inmates will get tired of all the cell time. Unfortunately, during lockdown tempers usually escalate, and the confinement provides time to plot new tactics of violence.

Our race representatives had all met and given each other empty assurances of no further violence. These promises are meant to pacify the administration and allow an unlock, but each side knows the pledges resemble ropes of sand. However, the warm sunlight felt pleasant on my skin, and my eyes feasted on majestic mountains. I gratefully inhaled the fresh desert air.

At the beginning and end of each time in the yard, most races gather in their self-designated area to say hellos and goodbyes. Coming off a long lockdown always creates tension. Neither side knows what the other is planning, so the groups stay tight at first, quiet and uncomfortable. Covert glances betray the confident appearance of many. As minutes passed, small groups mustered the courage to break out and walk the quarter-mile track. I was already at the baseball diamond, ready to get some exercise.

I had been praying during lockdown that God would intervene and allow us to move on without retaliation. I assumed my prayers had been answered and everything would be fine. Soon an hour passed. Then two. While playing right field, about thirty feet from the exercise bars that were claimed and occupied by the Black inmates, I noticed a once-loose group begin to tighten around the bars. *Am I imagining something*, I asked myself? Fear began to crawl up my spine as the possibility of violence clouded the sunny day. I tried to brush aside the apprehension, but it persisted. I began to talk silently to God and soon raised my hands toward heaven and spoke the words of Isaiah 54:17.

At last the inning was over, and I ran toward home plate. The group around the exercise bars hadn't moved. *It must have been my imagination*, I thought to myself. Then the gunner's voice boomed over the loudspeaker, "Equipment recall! Equipment recall!" We had ten minutes to say our goodbyes and return to the front of our housing units. As I finished my handshakes, out of the corner of my eye I caught a glimpse of an unusual movement and knew instantly that my hunch had been correct.

Running at full speed, a wall of angry faces was coming straight for me. I began to whisper the words "God help me." While the words were still on my tongue, the first wave attacked. I felt as if I were being swallowed alive. The flash of steel and blurred images of other homemade weapons made me pray and struggle ever harder. *If I can just stay standing,* I thought, *I might have a chance.* I heard and felt the fists pounding and wondered if I were being stabbed. The riot alarms blared as the gun-tower guards yelled over their loudspeakers, "Get down! Get down!" Then the unmistakable ear-shattering thunder of the riot guns added to the maelstrom.

These generally nonlethal guns shoot gas canisters and solid rubber blocks as an initial attempt to disperse the rioters. If they fail, guards shoulder their Mini-14 assault rifles, and then people die. Although it seemed like hours, the attack lasted only a few minutes before the mob retreated. With more than sixty Black inmates and only twenty White inmates, it didn't take long for the Blacks to exact the desired punishment.

Dazed and confused but still on my feet with way too much adrenaline in my body, I looked around. Suddenly I noticed a cop just feet away with his finger on the trigger of a giant bottle of pepper spray. With no further reason to stand and not relishing the thought of baking in the sun while coated with agonizing spray, I complied with the order to "get down!" Lying face down, spread-eagle, I was soon cuffed and ordered not to move.

The putrid smoke from hundreds of canisters hung like a blanket over the yard. Then came another unmistakable sound, the chilling crack and seldom-heard report of an assault rifle. I hoped it was a warning shot but couldn't tell. Four more times the menacing sound of death reverberated through the melee—then all fighting ceased. Police from all yards were still arriving in droves. Clothed in riot gear complete with helmets, shields, and guns, they formed lines and advanced shoulder to shoulder, handcuffing men as they inched along.

The sight seemed surreal—all around lay wounded, bloody men, some conscious, others not. The medical techs scurried from man to man, treating the worst injuries first with supplies from their bright-red emergency kits. The scene reminded me of a battlefield in a WWI movie. After bandaging a bleeding man next to me, a medical tech knelt down and asked, "How are you?" I didn't know. Everything was still attached and at the moment seemed to function. He rolled me over, then back, and said, "You're fine," as he scrambled to the next victim.

Finally the officers had everyone secured and began evacuating the most injured. Some went out on stretchers or wheelchairs, others limped and hobbled to the medical office for further attention. When nurses examined me thoroughly, they could find no apparent injuries from the beating other than a round spot on my back where I'd evidently caught a rubber bullet. Puzzled, they sent me back to my cell.

Most of the others did not fare so well. When I exchanged accounts with my Christian celly, who had only minor cuts and scrapes, we knelt and praised God for His protection. I had felt the fists landing; I had heard the blows contacting my head and body—but where were the marks? I had seen the weapons and knew they'd been used, but where were the cuts?

Several times in the past five years, racial riots have erupted on my yard, but I had always been out of harm's way. Previously, I just missed a riot because a mix-up at the Canadian border had mysteriously delayed a scheduled visit from some friends. Another time, the staff decided to do a controlled unlock, calling only thirty inmates of each race out to the yard. My name wasn't called, and blood flowed that day. Each time I had remained safe in my cell. But I always wondered what would have happened if I'd been out during the riots.

I don't have to wonder anymore. God answered that question and a few others on a sunny September day last year. "No weapon forged against you will prevail." Praise God!

Chapter 33

A NEW MISSION FIELD

Kneeling with my cell mate, Salty, we gave thanks to God, our Protector, for His miraculous deliverance only a few hours before when we'd both been viciously attacked in the prison race riot. Replaying the traumatic experience of the morning, I could see plainly how supernatural and awesome God's protective hand had truly been. Little did I know what the next few months had in store or how God would work even greater miracles.

I had never had any kind of write-up for misconduct nor been involved in an altercation during all my years in prison. But now I'd been in the middle of a major race riot. I had no idea what would happen to me but assumed that since I was a victim, I'd be OK.

Early one morning about a week after the incident, the sound of our food port opening wakened me. I looked up and saw the floor officer pushing several large garbage bags through the slot. Seeing my puzzled look, he explained we needed to put all our belongings in the bags. When I asked why, he responded, "Because you can't take anything but a pair of boxers and a T-shirt to the hole."

"The hole!" I gasped. I couldn't believe I'd heard him correctly. "But why? What did I do?" I sputtered.

The guard shrugged, "Participation in a riot." And he left. *Participation in a riot? Do ducks participate during duck hunting season?*

Shaking our heads and grumbling, Salty and I started packing our belongings. Though C yard is a treacherous and violent place, it had been my home for five and a half years. Many men had come to know Christ, and I would miss the solid band of brothers I had learned to know and love. But frightening thoughts of the hole soon replaced those reflections. Officially named administrative segregation, ad seg has been called "the hole" for decades. Thoughts of dirt floors, clanging keys, groans, and screams filled my head. Having never been to a level-four hole, all I knew were horror stories that had filtered back to the main line—tales of unimaginable violence and abuse handed out by inmates and cops alike. I did know for sure that every time someone committed a violent act on our yard, he disappeared to the hole, never to be seen again.

Lord, God, please have mercy and protect Your children. Salty and I repeated this prayer while waiting to be taken to the hole. We pleaded with God to be kept together during our time there. All of the unknowns drove me to my knees many times that day. The devil fabricated vivid images and awful scenarios, and I battled to push them aside. A week earlier the inmates in the hole had killed a man because he used his fists instead of a knife on a child molester. The worst of the worst live there, and I was frightened.

Finally the cops arrived to escort us to ad seg. They took us first to the program office, where they asked us if we could live together in ad seg. We both nodded like bobblehead dolls. *Thank You, Lord,* I silently whispered. At least we knew we'd have each other to worship with and talk to. From the program office they escorted us out of C yard and down the long desolate path to ad seg. Nervously I asked my escorting officer, "What will happen to us?"

"All I know is all you Whites will be on 'walk-alone' with your cell mate."

Thank You, Lord, I again prayed silently. One of my biggest fears involved going to the tiny concrete enclosure used as an exercise area for the hole inmates. That's where the recent killing had taken place. Walk-alone meant that the only other person on the concrete yard would be Salty. Praise God!

The officer showed us to our cell, the door slammed shut, and we gazed around the bare cement box we now called home. It contained only two bunks containing ripped, stained mattresses with two sheets, two blankets, soap, and toilet paper. Standing in my socks, boxers, and T-shirt, I compared my last cell with this one. I hadn't realized how much I had then—books, paper, and pencil, for instance.

We made our beds still wondering what came next. But we did know that God had answered two of our requests already. We were together and were safe from the pressures and politics of other convicts. Walk-alone took care of that. Using one of my socks and a bar of soap, I began the first order of business—cleaning the cell. Although it didn't have a dirt floor or a bucket in the corner, it was filthy.

The officers in the hole seemed as jaded as the inmates. All wore special stab-proof vests, gloves, and slip-on face shields. Often, in the hole, men will "gas" the cops. First they mix a cocktail of feces, urine, and blood. When the tray slot opens for meals, the inmate tries to hit the face of the unaware officer. "Darting," another form of assault on the guards, involves blowguns and mini-bows made with paper and elastic from socks or boxer shorts. The dart and arrow tips are staples soaked in blood and feces. Hepatitis A, B, and C, AIDS, and other diseases can be transmitted in the blink of an eye. Having to put up with these threats every day desensitizes the officers. Their faces expressionless, they rarely acknowledged a greeting or question. After five days of asking, we finally received two towels, and it was amazing how happy receiving a simple towel made me.

On day six our beloved chaplain surprised us with a visit and an armload of books and a Bible. Another answered prayer. We had not sent for him; God did. After a short chat and a prayer, he left, but the books filled our hearts with joy. Salty and I worshiped, prayed, and sang songs to our God. Later that evening I heard a light tapping on the wall. I put my ear to the wall, listening—the tapping resumed. I walked to the front of my cell and said, "Yeah?" into the crack of the door.

A moment later I heard a faint voice, "Excuse me. Are you busy?"

"No," I replied.

"May I come over?"

"Yes," I said.

Next came a small line under my door. "Pull it," said the voice.

So I began reeling in a finely spun line and soon found a note tied to it. In the hole, communication is prohibited outside an inmate's race, especially since most had just come out of the same riot. I knew my neighbor wasn't White, so thought it strange he'd send me a note. I opened it, and in neat, tiny print, my neighbor, a Northern Mexican, wrote that he'd seen the chaplain at our door earlier that day. He wrote that he was a Muslim but read Christian books, too, and he wanted a Bible. Overjoyed, and recognizing this opportunity to witness, I scrawled a note letting him know I had two Bibles and would give him one the next morning when the tray slot opened for breakfast. For the next few weeks until he left, we wrote back and forth, sharing our hopes and faith, talking only through silent notes, careful not to offend any of the races, for we were supposed to be enemies.

Soon the gnawing feeling of terror disappeared to be replaced by a strength I had not felt before. Feeling like true soldiers, we came to a new understanding of God. The barren cell became home, and I found I didn't miss all the trappings of mainline life. Without the distractions of TV and radio, my days became filled with long periods of prayer and Bible study. I felt a closeness with Christ as never before and understood the concept of "less is more." It truly is.

One day an officer appeared with some papers and began reading the technical jargon found on all prison paperwork. "On or about the fifth day of September . . . involved in a racial riot . . . subsequently you are being given a serious 115 for the charge of participation in a riot."

"Hold on! We're being charged with something?"

"Yup," he tersely replied. And he turned on his heel and disappeared down the long hall.

I couldn't believe it. "How can they do this?" I wondered out loud. That night I prayed longer and harder than ever, pleading with God to bring this to an end. How could any kind of charges be substantiated? Had anyone in authority actually seen what had happened? Salty and I were victims!

Knowing that at this point these were only charges, I tried to relax and pray that God would bring justice. But in the shadows of my mind, Satan persisted in reminding me that just like my conviction of two murders was wrong, so this would be wrong too, and it was all God's fault. Over and over I rebuked Satan, quoting James 4:7, 8, "Submit yourselves, then, to God. Resist the devil, and he will flee from you. Come near to God and he will come near to you. Wash your hands, you sinners, and purify your hearts, you double-minded."

A week later I read a book in which the author expounded on the silence of Jesus while Pilate questioned Him. In the face of such a hugely mishandled and corrupt trial, Jesus stayed silent.

The next morning an officer came to the door. "I am the investigative employee assigned to your case. What do you have to say about the riot, and who would you like to call as witnesses?" Most inmates would now morph into Johnnie Cochran and Dick Tracy all at once, realizing this is a one-shot opportunity to beat the system and overturn a conviction. Using all their pent-up anger plus legal jargon gathered from years of replaying their own cases and listening to others, and using any scrap of TV drama they can remember, they spew out legal words and judicial terms from otherwise foul mouths in the hope of beating this grave injustice, which most are guilty of anyway.

But instead, I looked at him and said, "I'm innocent, and the Lord is my witness."

He smiled, as if to say "Don't waste my time," and asked the question again.

"You have my statement. That's it." I waved him away.

Salty walked to the cell door. "Make it two. That's all I've got to say."

With a look of disbelief, the officer walked away mumbling to himself and shaking his head. Salty and I felt energized by giving possibly the shortest defense in inmate history. We again asked God for justice.

Finally, six weeks after our arrival at the hole, our hearing date arrived. A guilty verdict would automatically sentence us to a minimum of four months' hole time and an additional three years of housing on a maximum-security yard designed for inmates with disciplinary problems. We wore confident smiles as an officer escorted us to the hearing office. My turn came first, and I sat before a paper-littered desk belonging to a sour-faced man with the unmistakable bars of a lieutenant.

"So," he grunted as he began shuffling papers, reading what I knew must be my file. "Anything you want to add?"

"No."

"OK then. I'm finding you guilty of participation in a riot, which is a class D offense. . . ." His voice droned on, but I wasn't listening.

"Guilty?" I butted in. "How?"

The lieutenant looked at the escorting officer and motioned him to take me away. "Next!" he barked.

I couldn't believe it! How could this have happened? I half whined and half prayed. Moments later when Salty returned to the cell, I knew from the look on his face that he'd met the same fate. After a time of stewing, we decided to kneel together to thank God for doing His will—but we asked Him if He'd mind letting us in on His plan. So that was it; we knew our fate and slowly began to deal with the unjust decision. A few more months in the hole, then a transfer to another maximum-security yard. Starting over again, new faces, a new home, new cops, but ultimately, God's will.

After we had been in the hole exactly two months, an officer woke us early and said we had to meet with "the committee." We dressed quickly and were taken to a large room. My escort instructed me to enter and take a seat. Six men with unfamiliar faces sat at a long table, but I recognized one of the nameplates: Warden. His face void of emotion, his eyes like steel, he finally spoke. "Mr. Fleck, you have a choice." My throat tightened, and my mouth felt full of cotton. The warden continued, "If you'd be willing to go to B yard and not screw up, I'll suspend your charges and nullify your disciplinary action."

Whoa—nullify what? . . . No disciplinary action . . . B yard? My mind struggled to put everything in place. Only a minute before, I had been guilty of participating in a riot, going to a hard yard full of knuckleheads and violence. The future looked scary and everything seemed vague and hazy. Not saying anything, just sitting and panning the faces, I must have looked lost.

A miracle! But it didn't seem real. The warden must have seen the expression of disbelief on my face. "Well, Fleck, do you want to stay here or go?"

Finally I could speak. "Is my celly getting the same offer?"

The warden looked at his assistant and then back at me. "I can't discuss his affairs with you. You say you're a Christian. Have a little faith."

With that I quickly answered, "OK."

"The officer will escort you to B yard within the hour. You are dismissed."

As I passed Salty in the hall, I winked. If anyone had seen us in the cell a few minutes later jumping, hugging, and slapping each other on the back, they'd have thought we'd just been given our parole papers. In a sense, I guess we had. B yard is a much less violent place, a softer yard, filled with men just doing time, not looking for trouble.

A couple hours later we watched the dreaded walls of the hole grow distant as we moved to our new home.

God is good. Not a single prayer went unanswered. So here we are. A new home, a new attitude, and a new mission field.

Chapter 34

UNBELIEVABLE
NUMBERS

C ell 201," said the floor cop, pointing to the upper tier as Salty and I shuffled off toward our new home. Landing on a new yard is always hard at first. Dressed in white jumpsuits with the big black letters AD SEG emblazoned on the back attracted hundreds of eyes following our every step. Knowing no one, I kept on a straight line, looking only at the door marked 201. Once inside, Salty and I put down our few belongings accumulated in the hole and offered a prayer of thanks to our Redeemer.

In the hole I had been given a book explaining Psalm 23 verse by verse. Reading it daily truly had helped me cope while in ad seg, my valley of the shadow of death. The promise of green pastures, overflowing cups, and goodness and mercy struck me as wonderfully poetic and prophetic because the contrast between the evil, hate, and smell of death in the hole and this new yard were like night and day. Even C yard, only a stone's throw away, seemed like another world.

B yard, although still level four, houses those who have decided life in prison is more than stabbing and slicing. It didn't take long for the Lord to begin laying blessing after blessing on me. I felt like a tourist landing in Hawaii for the first time with the blessings of the Lord accumulating like beautiful sweet-smelling leis piled on one after the other.

"Mista Fleck and Mista McGraw—how are ya'll doin'?" a familiar face with an even more familiar Southern accent greeted me at my cell window. Only a day had passed, and there stood the silvery-haired Southern Baptist chaplain with the wide-brimmed hat. His smile and unique Southern grace almost brought a tear to my eye—God bless him!

He stood at our cell door smiling, as always, and then broke into his analogies of God's providence. "Boys," he began, "I have been doin' this for fifty years, and I have never seen the likes of such miracles as with you. Mista Fleck, you're now on B yard, and it ain't by chance. Without the hand of the Lord in your case, you should still be in the hole or shipped off down the road. But He's got work for you here. I want you to write a proposal for a discipleship group like ya'll had on C yard. Then send it to me, and I'll make it happen." I stood nodding my head, wanting to pinch myself to make sure his request was for real. We had prayer together, and off he went, leaving me with joy and the overwhelming feeling that B yard would be something special. The Spirit would soon move mightily.

I spent the next couple of weeks meeting the other Christian brothers, but I had problems. Since coming to B yard, I had lost my A_1A (A-one-A) status. Let me explain. Prison classifications fall into various types such as race (as I mentioned earlier), crime classification exacted in levels one through four, and job status. Job status is a big one, and most inmates will do and say just about anything to secure a job. On C yard I worked as the barber, but since the riot and trip to the hole, my work status had been revoked, throwing me back into the pool of nonwork-approved inmates.

It had taken eighteen months to secure the barber job on C yard back in 1998 before the major budget cuts in California. At that time High Desert State Prison ran a vocational program including painting, horticulture, masonry, engine repair, and many others. With vocational training and support services (janitors, kitchen workers, and clerks), about two-thirds of the men had jobs. When someone left the yard, his job was reassigned to the next inmate in line.

But the budget crunch ended all the vocational assignments, leaving hundreds of men jobless, stuck in their cells. A_1A, the classification for an assigned inmate, brings chances of a job and much more freedom. Workers get out of their cells every day, get yard every day for exercise and visiting, can make unlimited phone calls, get paid eight to thirty-two cents an hour, and are eligible for good-time credit, which reduces their sentence by about a third. Working completes a prisoner, often giving back a little self-respect and dignity.

But upon arrival at prison, all inmates are assigned A_2B, or fish status for short. They have limited yard access, one phone call a month, and no good-time credits; they are basically just shelved and warehoused like giant human cocoons waiting for the little white piece of paper or ducat telling of a job, an opportunity to blossom, and freedom, in a sense.

So now, even though I lived on a basically good yard, I went back to square one as far as job status. Knowing how the system worked, I prayed daily for God to open a door allowing me a reclassification.

Because of lack of access to the yard, I found it difficult to initiate the religious programs I believed were waiting to be enjoyed. *Lord, I really need to have access to the chapel. I need access to the brothers. Lord, please, if it is Your will, grant my prayer.* This prayer and similar prayers went up daily.

Each building has a "counselor," usually an ex-officer with no counseling training, so "case worker" would be a more-accurate job title. One day I walked past the office and noticed a familiar face. "Hey, there, Hanlon." I grinned. "Mind if I step in for a minute?"

"No, no, Fleck. C'mon in and sit down," he smilingly replied.

Hanlon, a friendly man, had been my counselor on C yard but now, coincidentally, was my counselor on B yard. Sort of a woodsy outdoors type, he loved to fish and hunt, and he dressed always in khakis, looking like he'd come straight out of an Eddie Bauer shop. He adorned his office with pictures of big game trophies. Knowing I am Canadian, he'd grill me on all the prime hunting and fishing locations, telling me of his plans to head north and find some big game. I figured he could pull some strings and find me a job. After some small talk, I asked him. His smile faded and almost apologetically he told me that since I have a life sentence and am ineligible for half-time, it could be three to five years or more before I'd be assigned a job.

His words stung as he explained the dilemma of a thousand inmates but only a couple hundred jobs. Lifers were at the back of the line, the bottom of the list, and nothing could be done. Saying goodbye, I left his office feeling so dejected, questioning God and His plan.

How quickly I forgot that only days earlier He'd delivered me from what appeared to be a long-term situation in ad seg. God didn't lead the Israelites through the desert to the Promised Land and then abandon them. Neither would He transfer me miraculously and then abandon me. Patience, patience, patience. I decided to exercise faith and submit the proposal for a discipleship group with the names I had gathered. In talking to the brothers, I noticed a negative vibe. Some were excited. Others explained they'd tried several times to begin a group, but it never materialized.

This yard contained many Christians and with that comes just as many doctrines. Each man seemed intent on Bible bashing others into agreeing with his convictions. With huge rifts and schisms created by this method, some of the brothers refused to speak to each other. Having never encountered this difficulty before, I felt uneasy and at a loss on how to solve it. A few of us prayed together, asking God to solve the problem—and as always, He did. About a month later I met with Chaplain Green and learned the proposal had been approved, but strangely, instead of granting permission for a "discipleship group," we had permission to organize a "prayer meeting."

As I read the heading, a light went on: A Holy Spirit–prompted moment of clarity revealed the solution to our problem. How could doctrines drive wedges between the believers if no one discussed them? Prayer—that was the answer. I felt a rush of excitement knowing *He* again had done as He had promised. While there I noticed the absence of any clerk and saw the empty office where inmates usually worked. "Chaplain Green, would you like me to help out in here? I am familiar with how to do the church lists because I did them on C yard as a volunteer."

He hemmed and hawed for a minute, then asked, "Are you assigned any place?"

"No," I replied.

"So you're A_2B then?"

"Yes," I admitted.

"I can't bring you in because workmen's comp doesn't cover A_2B's. Sorry, Fleck. I'd love to have you, though—matter of fact, I'll fill out the paperwork and see what the brass say. It's their call."

A spark of hope reignited my faith, and I left the chapel. *Lord, it's up to You. I know You'll find a way,* I prayed silently to my Companion and Savior.

A few days later the Medical Technical Assistant (MTA) dropped off medications for Salty. He glanced at me and asked, "Fleck, is there any reason why you're not working?" Stunned at his out-of-the-blue question, I told him I'd been put back to A_2B status waiting for an assignment.

He paused and then asked, "Would you like a job as the clinic porter?"

"Would I? You bet I would!" I jumped up and added, "Please, if you help me get that job, that would be great!"

He nodded, "Let me see what I can do, Fleck."

"Wow, a job as the clinic porter," I thought out loud.

Salty couldn't believe it. "Skip, if that happens, I know the Lord's looking out for you, man."

Clinic porter is a plum job, one of the best on the yard. One advantage includes working during facility lockdowns. While a thousand guys sit in their cells waiting for an unlock, the porter in the clinic always works. Also, only one inmate works in the clinic, so he won't be fired for someone else's thievery or stupidity. *Oh boy, if I could get that job and have Sabbaths off, it would be a dream.* These and many other thoughts circled through my mind.

About noon my door popped open and the words, "Fleck, go to the clinic," boomed over the loudspeaker. My heart rate doubled as I hurriedly pulled on my pants and boots, grabbed my ID card, and hustled out. At the clinic the MTA said, "I called inmate assignments, and the lieutenant is considering hiring you. But," he warned, it may not happen 'cause you're A_2B with a whole yard full of guys ahead of you on the list."

I looked at him and the officer standing behind him and said, "I prayed for a job, and God is going to answer my prayers with a job here—just watch." Looking around I noticed the clinic floor hadn't seen a mop or broom for quite some time, so I asked if I could go ahead and clean up a bit.

"Sure, knock yourself out," he replied. Two hours later, with sweat pouring down my face, I had the place shining. Then I asked the medical assistant if he'd heard anything about my job ducat. He shook his head and said No. I walked home, prayed again, and waited. At 6:00 P.M. that night, the floor officer stopped at my door. Seconds later a small square piece of white paper slid under it. "Thank You, God. Thank You so much," I said as I picked it up. "Your job assignment is clinic porter," I read and reread with tears in my eyes. Some men had been waiting years without even a whisper of a job. But God put me where He wanted me in less than a month and a half. Thank You, Lord.

But the miracle doesn't end there. The very next day, as I finished my morning cleaning in the clinic, the chaplain called me to the chapel just a few doors down. When I arrived, he smiled, handed me a square card, and said, "Read it."

It looked like a business card, but it said "Volunteer Chapel Clerk" with the captain's signature in big blue letters scrawled along the bottom. I could not believe what I was seeing. Only the day before, I was A_2B, had no job, and knew about eight hundred guys were ahead of me on the list. Today, praise God, I had two jobs.

In that moment, I heard the Spirit saying, *"If you're patient, I can do all things."* I began thinking how easy it will be when the time is right for the Holy Spirit to grant my habeas corpus appeal by softening the court's heart. I couldn't help but think that in many respects, my impatience, my selfishness, and my unwillingness to listen had hindered what the Holy Spirit intends to do. And by comparing my own wilderness experience of disobedience, I can see how it parallels to the children of Israel's years of travel in the desert. How much longer until I am granted access to freedom? In many ways I think it depends on me and just how willing I am to let God do *His* will in me.

Chapter 35

PRISON

HIJINKS

Prison—the word connotes gloomy cells, angry inmates, and total despair. But perhaps surprisingly, bits of humor and a little lighthearted fun coexist with the bleakness.

I had a neighbor named Ron who, it seemed, thrived on pushing the cops to their limits. Always looking for ways to disrupt their days, he'd plan his attacks meticulously.

Each day we walk a short hundred yards to the chow hall for meals. Once inside, we line up and take our trays from a hole in the wall. It's not a cafeteria. We get whatever is put on our trays, which includes an apple every evening, the only fruit ever served. Apples are prized, as they are the main ingredient in homemade wine. Since we are not permitted to take food from the chow hall, every evening a game of cops and robbers is played. We stuff apples in our socks, pants, and shirts; and the cops, knowing we're packing, form two lines right outside the doors exiting the hall. Five or six cops will pat down as many as they can, but the majority slip by, laughing all the way to their cells. Day in and day out—this is the scene.

High Desert also has another problem—one with wings and a mean targeting system. Seagulls. Rules forbid us to feed them so, of course, any self-respecting inmate goes out of his way to throw the gulls something at every opportunity. Gulls know about apples at chow time. Although fruit isn't their food of choice, like rats, they eat anything. But bread, wonderful soft bread, causes a frenzy as each gull tries to snatch a bite—much like sharks competing for chum.

When cops find fruit, they make it a point to toss it a fair distance to avoid any gull matter dropping their way. But more than once, I've heard the unmistakable volley of expletives as a bird hits its target.

Day after day Ron tried stealing apples, and every time he'd get caught. Then one night he tapped me on the shoulder and said, "Skip, watch this." Breaking his bread into tiny pieces, he filled his back pocket until it bulged. Then we filed out and, as always, a gauntlet of eagle-eyed cops waited to foil the nightly attempts. Ron didn't make it five steps before a young cop pulled him over. With a look of disdain but a hint of mischief in his eyes, Ron assumed the posture of a frisk, and the cop began a pat down. Seeing the bulge in Ron's back pocket, he quickly looked inside. "What are you trying to do stealing bread?" he barked as if he'd just cracked an international smuggling ring.

Ron, in a combative voice, quickly replied, "I ain't got no bread!" These words simply acted like a springboard to aggravate the cop, who immediately reached into the pocket and yanked out a handful.

Holding the bread like a trophy, the cop then threw it to the ground at Ron's feet and growled, "Get out of here!" But the cop failed to notice the twenty or so pairs of beady eyes now riveted on a fresh mound of bread crumbs directly in the center of the gauntlet. At once I saw the perfectly engineered plan, which included breaking the bread into tiny pieces so one gull couldn't carry it all away. As Ron and I looked over our shoulders, all we could see were wings, feathers, and ducking cops amid the screeching, frenzied attack. It was a work of art, enough to send us into gales of laughter all the way home. The cops could only hope for the best as the winged rats exacted a punishment by proxy on our behalf.

Chapter 36

SINGING
FROM PRISON

At times I feel strange when I write about God and all His blessings in prison.

Strange, in a way, that I perceive people may think I'm sugar coating my situation. I couldn't possibly be OK within those walls, living with "those kind of people." Yet "those kind of people" are my brothers, with whom I know I'll spend eternity. It's the Bible-given and Spirit-confirmed knowledge that makes me OK day after day.

Just yesterday as I exercised, the endorphins kicked in, as well as the zeal. I had to quit for a minute to thank God for my experience in the hole. In an odd way, I actually miss the fear I felt there. That fear pushed me so close to God. But now I seem to be talking to Him from a distance instead of being cradled in His arms. I want to talk to Him in whispers out of closeness, not petitions out of need.

I know He hasn't gone anywhere. It's me and my do-it-myself, independent, self-centered flesh that I struggle with. Now I see it. Before the hole, I couldn't. Life behind bars is truly a blessing, and little by little over the years, I can see through dried tears that God allowed me to be in exactly the place I needed to be. Not because I'm guilty of murder, but because I'm a slow learner. Time is something I need in order to understand my incredibly wicked self and learn to know my incredibly merciful God.

If everyone could experience God's hand of protection when faced with danger, lives would change. My experiences are minor compared to the true courage of those in oppressed countries where owning a Bible could mean death. But to me, they have been life-changing.

I hope people will believe me when I say life isn't boring, mundane, or listless in prison or anywhere, if God is in the driver's seat. Those without hope of Christ's coming will always feel that life is bleak. I've been there. I know. But every day God brings opportunities. If I'm focused on my own agenda and myself, I will miss those beautiful windows of opportunity, whether God gives me the opportunity to witness or whether God simply cracks His window and calls, "Skip, I've got a surprise for you. Want it?"

"Oh, Lord my God, I want it. I want every nugget, every surprise, every moment I can spend with You and only You." But as soon as my eyes wander, the window shuts, and usually He makes me aware of the opportunity lost. It's agonizing to realize I stood Him up. He was waiting, and I blew Him off. Lord, forgive me. Through it all, He has always waited patiently.

I want to be with my Father. I never want to miss any opportunities. They come in many different forms. One such opportunity is our dayroom. The buildings are built in a square with two tiers of cells around the perimeter, leaving the inside as one giant room. It's split in two parts, and each has a set of tables, benches, showers, and phone. We're allowed dayroom time every other evening. For an hour, while everyone else plays cards, hustles wares, or visits, a small group of believers meets at a table to spend some time with God. Talk about fulfilling! Each evening a different brother brings a short message. We have opening and closing prayer, all in the midst of noisy chaos. Tables on every side, loud voices, gambling, cussing. But our little flock lifts up praises to Christ.

One night Sammy, a Romanian Pentecostal brother, began talking about the gift of tongues. He believes that without this gift, no one can be saved. I had to pray just to keep my mouth shut and not argue with him. But, thank God, I'm learning.

We've been through discussions about the state of the dead and the destruction of the wicked, and we have come to an understanding that we can disagree and still be brothers. I prayed for God to keep my argumentative self quiet for a change.

Sammy went on and on, and just when dayroom time was almost over, I asked him to read 1 Corinthians 12:11 and 22:7–30. About that time another brother confirmed the point. Just like that, the conversation came to a calm close, we all shook hands, and we hugged each other, thanking one another for new insights.

Another opportunity comes in the chapel. With my job I have full access to the chapel, and the potential for new programs is unlimited. I say "potential" because all functions inside the chapel demand, for security reasons, that a staff member be present. This person can be any full-time staff member or a volunteer. With the proposal for a prayer meeting granted by Chaplain Green, the last hurdle involved finding a volunteer.

While walking the track one day, I noticed a man in street clothes standing in front of my building. As I neared, I recognized the unmistakable smile of Jerry W. I shook his hand, hugging him like a long-lost friend. Jerry had visited two years previously while I still lived on C yard, but due to some scheduling problems and other commitments, he could not help our prison ministry then. After some small talk, he said, "Skip, I've just received a chaplain's card and have been cleared to help out here."

I was shocked! We needed a volunteer, and not two days before, we had all prayed God would provide a man to help us. Jerry had no knowledge of our prayer group or our need of a volunteer. But God sent him. Praise God!

After clearing my head and catching my breath, I went on to explain that coincidentally or not, we had been approved to run prayer meetings but needed a volunteer. He sounded as excited as I, and we were soon discussing the details. It's officially listed as "SDA prayer meeting" on the schedule, and I rejoiced that Jesus had opened the doors to make it happen.

Twenty men signed up for our first meeting. Knowing the past problems of arguments between brothers, I felt nervous and worried that the meeting could get ugly. I prayed that the Spirit would silence the evil one's attempts to ruin our fledgling group. The time came and soon twenty smiling faces made their way to the chapel, where Jerry greeted each one at the door. To avoid the misconception that anyone would be getting preachy, we arranged the chairs in a circle. I had printed a brief overview of the group's purpose and handed a sheet to each man. My heart pounded, and I continued to pray silently as the men read the handout. It said:

Prayer Meeting
- **One requirement**   Jesus Christ is your Lord and Savior
- **One teacher**   The indwelling Holy Spirit
- **Purpose of group**   Bring about change through prayer
   Strengthen each other for evangelism
   Practice servanthood and discipleship

Group Format
- **Song**   Two worship songs
- **Prayer**   Special requests
   Pray in a circle, one at a time
- **Testimony of the Week** One or two share answered prayers
- **Message (time permitting)** Given by a different brother weekly
   Speaker has the floor—NO interruptions

Brotherly Commitment to the Group Read 2 Timothy 2:14, 23–25; Titus 3:9

All brothers have made a public commitment to avoid controversial doctrine and to remember the goal—feed the sheep and evangelize nonbelievers.

It seemed as if a collective sigh of relief went out as each one read the overview. Because previous attempts to have meetings resulted in one brother assuming the pulpit and hammering his doctrine into others, everyone had understandably been guarded and uneasy. But our format left no opportunity for hidden agendas. We followed our format, and soon the Spirit took over, and a life-changing meeting occurred. Red and yellow, black and white poured their hearts out one by one. Sobs, hallelujahs, amens, and "Say it louder, brother!" sounded through the circle. Our prayers took so long we didn't have time for a message, and that was just fine. An hour and a half later, twenty changed men left the chapel, a glorious experience!

In the weeks that followed, attendance grew. Soon sixty men came, sat in a circle, and prayed, one by one waiting for the Spirit's hand and moving grace. Sometimes if Jerry could not attend, the sergeant stationed a cop at the back. I wonder what went through his mind as he watched and heard men pray for him and his co-workers. During these times of prayer, many decided to commit fully to God by signing up for baptism. We started a tithing system so the brothers could assist indigent inmates. Our little flock took a collection and on Christmas Eve handed out cookies, licorice, and messages of hope written on paper to every cell in one block. Even the most hardened convicts gave us a nod, a thank you, and a merry Christmas wish. (I've never forgotten how the Lord used a box of candy twelve years earlier to coax me back.)

Thirteen years—has it been that long? Yes, it has. Oh what a powerful God I serve. Many times I have contemplated Psalm 37, as so many of the passages seem to reflect my life. Here is my application:

Verse 1:
> Do not fret because of evil men
> > or be envious of those who do wrong.

Killers surround me, but I feel safe.

Verse 2:
> For like the grass they will soon wither,
> > like green plants they will soon die away.

A constant stream of men stab or get stabbed, are here today and gone tomorrow. But the Christian brothers persevere and walk the yard every day, watching and waiting patiently for opportunities to share Jesus.

Verse 3:
> Trust in the LORD and do good;
>> dwell in the land and enjoy safe pasture.

Does it get any plainer? Trust and do good and enjoy a safe pasture. No weapon formed against me shall prosper; I have experienced this promise firsthand.

Verse 4:
> Delight yourself in the LORD
>> and he will give you the desires of your heart.

It's one of my favorite texts in Psalms. Many have written commentaries on this verse. Let me give you mine. Life has many pitfalls no matter which side of the wall you're on. Desires can be pitfalls, but they can be pure and beautiful too. Within my world, the world I've tried to paint for you, I honestly do have the desires of my heart. It would be silly for me to tell you I don't wish for physical freedom someday. But due to bad choices in the past, prison is now my world. Oh God, You are so full of mercy.

Friends, I do have the desires of my heart within the parameters in which I live. Here's the key to this text: If I delight myself in the Lord, He will become the desire of my heart. God has chosen me to serve. I can give tiny cups of cold water to travelers in this parched wasteland drawing always from the cool, never-ending supply unknown to most. I am in need of nothing; God has provided every physical need but, more important, every spiritual need as well. He's given me peace in the midst of chaos, love in the midst of hate, and joy in the midst of much loneliness and pain. This verse is an unparalleled promise. King David, whose life was filled with trauma, knew the secret to true happiness, and it is Jesus Christ.

Verses 5 and 6:
> Commit your way to the LORD;
> > trust in him and he will do this:
> He will make your righteousness shine like the dawn,
> the justice of your cause like the noonday sun.

Righteousness and justice are the foundation stones of God's throne. When He tells me to trust in Him after all the proof He's given me of His love, mercy, and protection, I must obey. Oh, if only you who are reading this would fully grasp the depth of His desire to be a part of your lives. If only you and I would stop trying to run things ourselves and become pliable again, He will be our righteousness, and justice will prevail.

Verse 7:
> Be still before the LORD and wait patiently for him;
> > do not fret.

I ask You, Lord, to please sear these verses into the depths of our minds. Play these words back every time we fail, every time we decide the world has something to offer. You and You alone, Lord, are the strength, the justice, and the righteousness. It is only by Your grace that breath sustains our fleeting lives. Lord, I beg You, fill the hearts of Your servants with a desire to delight themselves in You so You can show them the blessings waiting to be lavished abundantly. And one more thing, Lord. Thank You. Thank You for giving me the desires of my heart. Amen, and God bless.
Skip

Rick, age sixteen months

Rick, age seven

Rick, his dad, and older brother, Rod

Rick and Rod showing their horses

Rod and Rick

Rick, age sixteen

Rod, Rick, and their parents,
Marlene and Llewellyn Fleck

Rick's high-school graduation

Rick and his parents at the
California coast

Rick's house in Menifee, California

Rick at his trial, December 1996

Rick working as a pitchman in Calgary

Kenny Smith with Rick's dad

Jesse and his bride

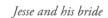

Cyril and Lyn Connelly

Rick with his parents

Rick and Rod